Contents

Designed and published by the Wales Tourist Board, Brunel House, 2 Fitzalan Road, Cardiff CF2 1UY.
Written by Roger Thomas Freelance Services.
Printed by The Westdale Press.
Colour reproduction by Scanagraphics Ltd.
Typesetting by Folio Graphics Ltd.
Copyright © 1996 Wales Tourist Board.
ISBN 1 85013 071 X

D0301903

The rolling farmlands of Wales's border country

Accommodation Plus ...

This is more than an accommodation guide. It's a complete holiday planner, with information on Wales's countryside and coastline, its national parks and 'Areas of Outstanding Natural Beauty', its countless castles, craft workshops and attractions.

The great outdoors

Wales's fresh, green surroundings are an increasingly prized asset. It's a pleasant surprise to discover, in this day and age, that you can drive uninterrupted all the way from South to North Wales through a landscape of hills and mountains. Or that you can walk for almost 200 miles along a coast path in Pembrokeshire with only the seabirds for company.

There are no less than three national parks here – the Brecon Beacons, Pembrokeshire Coast and Snowdonia. There are even more official 'Areas of Outstanding Beauty' – the Clwydian Range, Gower Peninsula, Isle of Anglesey, Llŷn Peninsula and Wye Valley. And 40 per cent of Wales's 750-mile seashore has been designated as untouched Heritage Coast.

Attractions and activities

This great natural beauty is a backcloth for all kinds of things to see and do. Wales's rich history is reflected in atmospheric medieval castles and walled towns. Its vibrant artistic and cultural life is expressed at folk festivals and craft workshops.

The country is a stimulating mix of traditional and innovative – old slate caverns have been revitalised as tourist attractions, there are narrow-gauge railways and a unique 'village of the future' dedicated to conservation. And on the activities front, Wales offers everything from walking to watersports, pony trekking to mountain biking.

Llanberis Lake Railway

2

Visit a pottery or craft workshop on your travels

Brecon Beacons National Park

Green Wales

Point to any part of Wales on the map and you're likely to locate beautiful surroundings – rugged Snowdonia in the north, perhaps, or the high, wild country of the Cambrian Mountains in Mid Wales, or the grassy slopes of the Brecon Beacons in the south.

Wales is green from top to bottom. The quality of its environment is something special – and it intends to keep it this way. There's a wealth of precious, protected places in Wales's many national parks and nature reserves, 'Areas of Outstanding Natural Beauty' and country parks.

Snowdonia and the Brecon Beacons

These two national parks are very different in character. Snowdonia is a dramatic jumble of rocky outcrops, tumbling rivers, brooding moors and deep, wooded valleys. The Brecon Beacons, in contrast, are smooth, grassy and open, offering a rare sense of space and freedom.

The Snowdonia National Park takes its name from Snowdon, the highest mountain in England and Wales. It's a huge area of 845 square miles, extending southwards all the way to Machynlleth. The 519-square-mile Brecon Beacons National Park also covers a lot of ground, from the Wales/England border almost as far as Swansea.

Wild Wales, verdant vales

Wales's undisturbed rural heartlands lie in Mid Wales, an area of rolling border country, lakes and mountains. When people speak of 'Wild Wales' they refer to the remote wildernesses of Plynlimon and the Cambrian Mountains, or the silent hills and marshlands around Tregaron where the rare red kite has made its home, or the spectacular old drover's road that climbs across the 'roof of Wales' to Abergwesyn.

Wales also has its pastoral, sheltered side along valleys such as the lovely vales of Conwy and Clwyd in the north, and the Teifi and Towy in the south.

Areas of outstanding beauty

Possibly the loveliest valley of them all is the Wye Valley, an 'Area of Outstanding Natural Beauty' which runs northwards from Chepstow to Monmouth through thickly wooded hillsides. And in North Wales there's another AONB – the Clwydian Range, an exhilarating line of rounded hills standing guard over green border country and the rich farmlands of the Vale of Clwyd.

4

Llyn Gwynant, Snowdonia

Coasting Along

Wales's 750-mile coastline has something for everyone – lively resorts and secluded coves, salty old fishing villages and modern marinas, popular beaches and remote bays.

Porthdinllaen on the Llŷn Peninsula

Beside the seaside

For entertainment-packed seaside holidays, there's the sandy North Wales coast with its string of attractive resorts – elegant Llandudno and the colourful, happy-go-lucky appeal of Colwyn Bay, Rhyl and Prestatyn.

Along the Mid Wales coast, Aberystwyth is an attractive mix of Victorian and modern influences. Barmouth and Tywyn, with their fine beaches and mountain-backed settings, are also popular spots, while picturesque Aberdovey attracts sailors as well as holidaymakers.

South Wales's long coastline offers everything from all the fun of the fair at Barry Island and Porthcawl to stylish Saundersfoot and Georgian Tenby.

Away from it all

Wales's national parklands, 'Areas of Outstanding Natural Beauty' and Heritage Coast are made for the quieter style of seaside holiday. The Isle of Anglesey, fringed with vast dunes, rocky promontories and beaches, is dotted with charming little resorts like Rhosneigr, Beaumaris and Benllech.

Anglesey and the Llŷn Peninsula are official AONBs. Along Llŷn's spectacular shores you'll discover more splendid, secluded beaches, towering cliff scenery, and pretty places to stay such as Abersoch, Criccieth and Nefyn.

There's a grand sweep of coastline, from north to south, along Cardigan Bay. Here, you can get lost amongst the dunes of Shell Island near Harlech, or explore the coves and grassy headlands of Ceredigion's Heritage Coast (don't miss Mwnt, a little jewel, or the quaysides at New Quay and Aberaeron).

Pembrokeshire is another – and bigger – jewel. The Pembrokeshire Coast National Park is one of Europe's finest stretches of coastal natural beauty. Wherever you choose – Newport, Fishguard or St David's in the north, Newgale, Broad Haven or Dale in the west, Tenby or Saundersfoot in the south – you'll be amongst breathtaking coastal scenery.

There's more great beauty along the endless sands of Carmarthen Bay where Dylan Thomas sought his inspiration, and the magnificent Gower Peninsula. Gower's sheltered sandy bays and sea-cliffs enjoy a special status – the peninsula was the first part of Britain to be declared an 'Area of Outstanding Natural Beauty'.

Tenby harbour

An Eventful Year

Wales is an eventful place, with an wide-ranging programme of festivals and fairs, artistic and sporting gatherings running throughout the year. Wales's most traditional cultural festival is the *eisteddfod* (which means 'sitting together'). You can also listen to world-class jazz at Brecon and Llangollen, mix with international literary stars at Hay-on-Wye, enjoy a colourful countryside jamboree at Builth Wells, or take a trip back to Victorian times at Llandrindod Wells.

Here, we've listed just some of the events on offer, beginning with the main activities. More details are contained in the Wales Arts Season '96 brochure and general Events Wales list. Both are available free from Wales Tourist Board, Davis Street, Cardiff CF1 2FU.

End of May-end of December
Mid Wales Festival of the Countryside

A festival which brings together over 500 events taking place throughout beautiful Mid Wales – bird-watching, guided walks, arts and crafts, sheepdog trials, farm and garden visits. David Bellamy, a keen supporter, has called it 'the role model for sustainable tourism'. Tel (01686) 625384

24 May-2 June
Hay Festival of Literature

Hay-on-Wye, the borderland 'town of books', provides an ideal setting for this literary festival with an international reputation. Attracts leading writers, poets and celebrities. Tel (01497) 821217

9-14 July
Llangollen International Musical Eisteddfod

A colourful, cosmopolitan gathering of singers and dancers from all over the world perform in the beautiful little town of Llangollen. A unique festival first held in 1947 to help heal the wounds of war by bringing the peoples of the world together – 1996 is its 50th anniversary. Tel (01978) 860236

22-25 July
Royal Welsh Agricultural Show

Four days of fascination – and a show that attracts a wide audience to Builth Wells, not just from the farming community but from all walks of life. One of Wales's premier events, held in the heart of the country, covering all aspects of agriculture – and a lot more besides. Tel (01982) 553683

3-10 August
Royal National Eisteddfod

Wales's most important cultural gathering, dating back to 1176, and held at a different venue each year. A festival dedicated to Welsh, Britain's oldest living language, with competitions, choirs, concerts, stands and exhibitions. Translation facilities available. This year's event will be held at Llandeilo. Tel (01222) 763777

9-11 August
Brecon Jazz

The streets of Brecon come alive with the sounds of summer jazz. A great three-day international festival with a wonderful atmosphere, which attracts the top names from the world of jazz. Over 80 concerts by bands and solo artists held throughout the town, both indoors and in the open air. Tel (01874) 625557

17-25 August
Llandrindod Wells Victorian Festival

The Mid Wales spa town of Llandrindod Wells celebrates its Victorian past. The festival includes street theatre, walks, talks, drama, exhibitions and music – all with a Victorian flavour. Tel (01597) 823441

Events for Everyone

February
17
Wales v Scotland International Rugby Union, Cardiff Arms Park
26
Llandudno Beer Festival

March
1
St David's Day Concert, St David's Hall, Cardiff
8-10
Folk Weekend, Llanwrtyd Wells
16
Wales v France International Rugby Union, Cardiff Arms Park
26
Conwy Seed Fair

April
14
Welsh Festival of Dressage, Usk Showground
26-5 May
Holyhead Arts Festival

May
1-31
Wrexham Maelor Arts Festival, Wrexham
2-6
Women's Welsh Open, St Pierre Golf Club, nr Chepstow
3-6
Landsker Walking Festival, Narberth
4
Dee and Clwyd Festival of Music Choral Concert, Corwen
9-12
Euro Wales 96 (Inter-European Emergency Medical and Rescue Services Exhibition), Merthyr Tydfil
Llantilio Crossenny Festival
10-12
Llangollen International Jazz Festival

17-19
Mid Wales May Festival, Newtown
18
Man versus Horse Marathon, Llanwrtyd Wells
Ruthin Twinning Festival
25-1 June
St David's Cathedral Festival
25-2 June
Gŵyl Beaumaris Festival (also Craft Fair 25-28 May)
26-27
City of Swansea Show
27-1 June
International Animation Festival, Cardiff
Urdd National Eisteddfod (Youth Eisteddfod), Johnstown, nr Wrexham

June
8
Llangollen Choral Festival
19-23
Criccieth Festival of Music and the Arts
21-23
Gŵyl Ifan - Welsh Folk Dancing Festival, Cardiff and district
22-28
Barmouth to Fort William Three Peaks Yacht Race
22-29
Gregynog Festival, nr Newtown.
29
RAF St Athan At Home Day, St Athan, nr Barry.

July
5-7
Beyond the Border - The Welsh International Festival of Storytelling, St Donat's Castle, nr Llantwit Major
Morris in the Forest Festival (Morris dancing, forest walks, etc), Llanwrtyd Wells

6-13
Gŵyl Werin y Cnapan, Ffostrasol, nr Llandysul
11-20
Welsh Proms '96, St David's Hall, Cardiff
13-14
Mid Wales Festival of Transport, Powis Castle, Welshpool
Wales International Kite Festival, Monmouth
15-27
Gower Music Festival
20-27
Fishguard Music Festival
20-2 Aug
Musicfest - Aberystwyth International Music Festival and Summer School
21-28
Ian Rush International Soccer Tournament (youth soccer), Aberystwyth
29-4 Aug
Gŵyl Conwy Festival

August
4-10
Conwy River Festival
8-9
United Counties Show, Carmarthen
8-11
Mountain Bike Festival, Llanwrtyd Wells
10-11
Caergwrle Historical Festival, nr Wrexham
17-24
West Wales Celtic Watersports Festival, Milford Haven and Waterway
20-28 (provisional)
Vale of Glamorgan Festival, Vale of Glamorgan and Cardiff

24-31
Presteigne Festival of Music and the Arts
26
World Bog-Snorkelling Championships, Llanwrtyd Wells

September
6-13
Barmouth Arts Festival
13
Conwy Honey Fair
15-21
North Wales Music Festival, St Asaph
17-20
Welsh International Four Days of Walks, Llanwrtyd Wells
20-28
Tenby Arts Festival

October
1-31
Swansea Festival
12-20
Llandudno October Festival
17-20
Welsh International Four Day Cycle Ride, Llanwrtyd Wells
24-26
Abertawe Festival for Young Musicians, University College, Swansea

November
9-17
Welsh International Film Festival, Aberystwyth
15-24
Mid Wales Beer Festival, Llanwrtyd Wells

December
3
Royal Welsh Agricultural Winter Fair, Builth Wells

History and Heritage

Wales's past is etched in its landscape. In your travels, you'll come across prehistoric and Roman remains, mighty medieval castles, manor houses and mansions, and a fascinating industrial heritage.

Caerphilly Castle

Ancient stones and medieval strongholds

Skeletal Pentre Ifan Cromlech in Pembrokeshire's Preseli Hills is one of many prehistoric monuments scattered throughout Wales. Thousands of years later, the Romans left camps, roadways, an extraordinary amphitheatre and bath-house at Caerleon and unique gold mine at Pumsaint. But more than anything else, Wales is famous for its castles – mighty medieval monuments such as Caernarfon, Conwy and Caerphilly, as well as dramatic ruins like Carreg Cennen, Llandeilo and remote Castell-y-Bere hidden beneath Cader Idris.

Historic houses

History also lives on at Llancaiach Fawr, a restored Tudor manor house in the Rhymney Valley which recreates the times of the Civil War. You can glimpse into grand country houses at National Trust properties such as Plas Newydd on Anglesey, Welshpool's Powis Castle and Erddig near Wrexham (an unusual 'upstairs, downstairs' house). Dignified Tredegar House at Newport is another mansion with two sides to its personality – a glittering interior together with preserved servants' quarters.

Industrial memories

In Wales, you'll discover gripping monuments to the era of coal, slate, iron and steel. 'King Coal's' reign is remembered at places like the Big Pit Mining Museum, Blaenafon, and the Rhondda Heritage Park. North Wales's slate industry has a successful modern spin-off at the popular Llechwedd Slate Caverns, Blaenau Ffestiniog – and slate is again the theme at the Gloddfa Ganol Mine, also in Blaenau Ffestiniog, and Llanberis's Welsh Slate Museum.

At Your Service

Welcome Host

Service and hospitality are as important as good accommodation and good food. We attach top priority to customer care – which is what our 'Welcome Host' scheme is all about. Open to everyone from taxi drivers to hotel staff, the scheme places the emphasis on friendliness and first-class service.

Welcome Host is part of a fine tradition in Wales – a tradition embodied in the welcoming greeting of *croeso*. Look out for the Welcome Host certificate or badge – it's a sure sign of the best in Welsh hospitality and service.

A Taste of Wales

Good food is another important ingredient of any holiday. In Wales, you're in for a treat, for there's been an explosion of talent

on the cooking scene. Throughout the country – in restaurants and hotels, inns and bistros – talented chefs are preparing everything from traditional favourites such as *cawl* (a nourishing, hearty broth) to modern, imaginative dishes, often cooked with a lighter touch.

A sign of good taste

When you travel through Wales you'll see many establishments displaying the Taste of Wales-*Blas ar Gymru* plaque. The scheme was created to encourage and promote a distinctive culinary identity through the use of local ingredients as well as traditional and innovative Welsh recipes. Wales is fortunate to have such an abundant larder of fresh, local produce, including superb seafoods, top-quality Welsh lamb, and wonderful cheeses. Taste of Wales members must use Welsh ingredients, cook them in a competent and creative manner and offer Welsh hospitality with enthusiasm. And quality is being further encouraged through a grading scheme which will be introduced during 1996.

So Accessible

One of Wales's big advantages is its ease of access. It's only a few hours by road and rail from most of the UK's main centres. Travel to Wales doesn't take up much time or money, so you can enjoy your holiday or short break to the full. And when you arrive, you'll be back in the days when driving was a pleasure on traffic-free highways and byways.

By car

Travel to South and West Wales is easy on the M4 and onward dual carriageway systems. The A55 North

Wales coast 'Expressway' whisks traffic past the old bottlenecks, including Conwy. Mid Wales is easily reached by the M54 which links with the M6/M5/M1.

Driving around Wales is a delight, for most highways remain blissfully quiet and uncrowded apart from a few peak summer weekends.

By rail

Fast and frequent Great Western InterCity services run between London Paddington and Cardiff (via Reading and Swindon), taking only 2 hours. This hourly service (every half hour at peak times) also runs to Newport, Bridgend, Port Talbot, Neath and Swansea, with onward connections to West Wales. Fast InterCity trains also link London (Euston) with the North Wales coast, serving both Bangor and Holyhead, and Newcastle/York to South Wales.

In addition, Regional Railways operates a direct service from London Waterloo (via Woking and Basingstoke) to Cardiff and other main

stations in South and West Wales. Regional Railways also runs other services into Wales. There are convenient and comfortable 'Alphaline' trains to Cardiff (and other destinations in South and West Wales) from:
Manchester/the North West;
Brighton/Portsmouth/Salisbury/Southampton;
The West of England/Bristol;
Birmingham/Gloucester.
'Alphaline' also operates from Birmingham to Aberystwyth and other Mid Wales resorts via Shrewsbury.

A 'North West Express' service operates from Manchester to the North Wales coast and Holyhead via Crewe and Chester.

Exploring Wales by train is a delight. Scenic routes include the beautiful Heart of Wales line from Shrewsbury to Swansea, the Conwy Valley line from Llandudno Junction to Blaenau Ffestiniog, and the Cambrian Coast line, which runs along the mountain-backed shoreline from Pwllheli to Machynlleth and Aberystwyth.

Ask about the money-saving unlimited-travel Rover and Ranger fares, some of which include the use of bus services.

By coach

National Express provides a nationwide network of express coach services. Convenient services to Wales operate from London's Victoria Coach Station and from almost all other major towns and cities in England and Scotland.

Towns and resorts throughout Wales are, of course, connected by a whole range of local and regional services. Details from Tourist Information Centres and local bus stations. You can travel cross-country by the TrawsCambria service running between Cardiff and Bangor (via Aberystwyth). Within North and Mid Wales you can combine coach and rail services through unlimited-travel Rover and Ranger tickets (see 'By rail' for details).

Further information

Please see 'Further Information' at the back of this guide for rail and coach travel information offices, plus details of sea and air services to Wales.

MILEAGE CHART

	MILES	JOURNEY TIME BY CAR
Birmingham – Aberystwyth	125	2 hrs 49 mins
Canterbury – Cardiff	219	3 hrs 56 mins
Coventry – Barmouth	133	2 hrs 51 mins
Exeter – Swansea	161	2 hrs 25 mins
Leeds – Llandudno	131	2 hrs 3 mins
London – Cardiff	155	2 hrs 40 mins
London – Tenby	245	4 hrs 7 mins
Manchester – Caernarfon	110	1 hr 58 mins
Nottingham – Swansea	202	3 hrs 10 mins
Peterborough – Aberystwyth	208	4 hrs 30 mins
Newcastle-upon-Tyne – Llandudno	230	3 hrs 56 mins
Reading – Carmarthen	177	2 hrs 40 mins
York – Welshpool	155	2 hrs 55 mins

Where to Stay

The remainder of this guide is filled with a great choice of places to stay. It covers all forms of self-catering – cottages, apartments, family complexes and caravan holiday home parks (including touring caravan and camping parks).

You can make your choice in confidence, because the accommodation featured – from the remotest cottage to the largest holiday complex – has been thoroughly checked out by a visit from one of our approved inspectors. Not only that, but we also clearly spell out the quality and standards for you.

Self-catering properties - Dragon grades for good quality

The DRAGON GRADES are your guide to QUALITY. They range from Grade 1 (simple and reasonable) to Grade 5 (exceptionally high quality). The grades reflect the overall quality of furnishings and decoration, <u>not</u> facilities. So a small cottage can achieve a top grade if what it offers, although limited in range, is of a very high standard.

Standard   Approved   Good   Very Good   Excellent

Two-centre self-catering holidays

See more of Wales on a two-centre self-catering holiday organised by the Welsh Association of Self-Catering Operators. Take your pick from an attractive range of properties located throughout Wales, in the national parks, along the coast, or away from it all in peaceful rural surroundings.

Details from: WASCO Two-Centre Holidays, PO Box 1316, Barmouth LL44 2ZA

Caravan holiday home parks – Two signs of quality

Our Dragon Award is given to INDIVIDUAL caravans. The 'Q' for quality grading scheme applies to the complete HOLIDAY HOME PARK – in short, two quality-based schemes which encourage high standards and help you to choose with confidence.

Dragon Award for individual caravans

Dragon Award caravans are something special, with features such as colour TV and heating at no extra charge. Look out for the distinctive Dragon Award symbol on the following pages.

Whatever you choose, you can be sure of standards, for caravans without Dragon Awards have also been inspected to ensure that they provide comfortable levels of accommodation.

'Q's for quality holiday home parks

All parks in this guide are part of the national 'Q' grading scheme. The grades reflect the overall standards of quality, <u>not</u> facilities. So a small park can achieve a top grade if what it offers, although limited in range, is of a very high standard.

Standard   Approved   Good   Very Good   Excellent

Touring caravan and camping parks

There's an excellent choice of well-equipped and well-managed parks in attractive locations throughout Wales. Again, quality is assured, for all parks in this guide participate in the 'Q' grading scheme.

Accommodating wheelchair users

 Accessible to a wheelchair user travelling independently

 Accessible to a wheelchair user travelling with assistance

 Accessible to a wheelchair user able to walk a few paces and up a maximum of three steps

For further details, please see 'Information for visitors with disabilities' in the 'Further Information/Useful Addresses' section of this guide.

Tenby on the Pembrokeshire coast

Making Your Booking

Book direct

Telephone or write to the place of your choice direct. It's as simple as that. If you phone, please check the prices and follow up the call with a letter of confirmation enclosing whatever deposit you've agreed with the proprietor.

Prices

For self-catering accommodation (furnished properties and caravan holiday home parks) rates are PER UNIT PER WEEK.

For touring caravan and camping parks, rates are for TWO PEOPLE and their caravan, motorhome or tent PER NIGHT.

All prices quoted include VAT at the current rate (17$\frac{1}{2}$%). Prices and other specific holiday information in this guide were supplied to the Wales Tourist Board during June–September 1995. So do check all prices and facilities before confirming your booking.

Book through a TIC

Look out for this symbol on the following pages. It means that you can book the featured accommodation through any networked Tourist Information Centre. Please see the TIC list at the back of this guide for more details on this Bed Booking Service.

i

Deposits

Most operators will ask for a deposit when a reservation is being made. Some establishments may request payment in advance of arrival.

Cancellation and insurance

When you confirm a holiday booking, please bear in mind that you are entering a legally binding contract which entitles the proprietor to compensation if you fail to take up the accommodation. It's always wise to arrange holiday insurance to cover you for cancellation and other unforeseen eventualities. If you have to alter your travel plans, please advise the holiday operator or proprietor immediately.

Looking after your best interests

We care about our visitors' views and encourage you to make any comments you may have about your stay to the proprietor of the establishment at the time of your visit. In this way it may be possible to make your stay even more pleasurable and to arrange for new facilities and services to be provided in the future. If you need to get in touch with the Wales Tourist Board about any aspect of your stay please write to the Visitor Services Unit, Wales Tourist Board, Davis Street, Cardiff CF1 2FU. We will let you have a reply to your letter within 15 working days of its receipt.

Key to Symbols

SC	Self-Catering
SCA	Self-Catering Agencies
CP	Caravan Holiday Home Park
TC	Touring Caravan and Camping Park
	Recipient of the Wales Tourist Board Dragon Award
	Welcome Host (minimum of 50% of staff trained)
P	Private car parking/garage facilities for guests' use
	Dogs/pets accepted on the premises by arrangement
	Licensed club or bar on the park
h	All rooms in all units have fixed heating
h	Some rooms in all units have fixed heating
	TV in each unit
	Indoor heated swimming pool on site/park
	Outdoor heated swimming pool on site/park
X	Cafe or restaurant on park
	Washing machine/launderette available
SP	Special weekend/midweek or short break holidays, including Christmas or New Year available
	Foodshop/mobile foodshop on park
M	Extra charge for gas/electricity/solid fuel
	Bed linen provided free of charge
	Bed linen available for hire
	Evening entertainment on park
	Electric hook-ups available
	Advance booking necessary in peak season
	Showers on park
	Butane or propane gas available on park
i	Accommodation may be booked through Networked Tourist Information Centres
	Railway Station

Please note: The symbols, together with the descriptive wording in the following accommodation advertisements, have been provided by the proprietors.

Using This Guide

Please note that the borders between each area are only approximate. Places on or close to the border may choose to be listed under the area or areas of their choice.

It's easy to find your way around this guide. The rest of the book is filled with 'where to stay' information presented as follows. Firstly, we divide the accommodation up into Wales's 12 holiday areas (see the map and index opposite). Then within each individual area, the resorts, towns and villages are listed alphabetically. Each place has a map reference enabling you to pinpoint it on the detailed gridded maps at the back of the book.

Holyhead

1

Beaumaris

Llangefni

Menai
Bridge

Llanfairpwllgwyngyll

This island is a place of great natural beauty, history and heritage. The coastline is astonishingly varied – from the dunes of Newborough to the sea-cliffs of Holyhead Mountain and the open sands of Red Wharf Bay. Anglesey, with its small, stylish resorts, is the perfect destination for the quieter seaside holiday.

If you can drag yourself away from the beach you'll find a huge range of places to visit – ancient burial chambers, the mansion of Plas Newydd, Beaumaris Castle and the award-winning Anglesey Sea Zoo to name but a few. If you're a birdwatcher, bring your binoculars to the cliffs at South Stack or the sands at Malltraeth. For sailors, there are the sheltered waters of the Menai Strait between Anglesey and the mainland of North Wales.

It's a fact...

Thomas Telford's elegant Menai Suspension Bridge connecting Anglesey to mainland Wales was opened in 1826. The nearby Britannia Bridge, which carries road and rail traffic, dates from 1850. Most of the island's 125-mile coastline has been declared an 'Area of Outstanding Natural Beauty' (designated in 1966). The world-famous town with the longest name is Llanfairpwllgwyngyllgogerychwyrndrobwllllantysiliogogogoch, which means 'St Mary's (Church) by the white aspen over the whirlpool, and St Tysilio's (Church) by the red cave'. Locals make do with Llanfairpwll.

Ae3 Beaumaris

Beautifully sited Anglesey coastal resort with splendid 13th-century castle. Other historic buildings along main street, Victorian Gaol, enchanting Museum of Childhood, fascinating old courthouse, and Beaumaris Marine World. Yachting centre with golf course and excellent fishing. 16th-century Penmon Priory nearby. Ideal touring centre for Snowdonia with superb views of mountains across Menai Strait.

Ac1 Bull Bay

Pretty little harbour and sands on rugged north coast of Anglesey. Golf course on slopes overlooking sea. Close to Cemaes Bay, another picturesque little port, and the old harbour town of Amlwch. Magnificent cliff scenery along this quiet, unexplored stretch of coast.

Ad3 Llangefni

Market town and shopping centre, Anglesey's administrative 'capital'. Fine touring base; almost all of the island's coastline is within 10–15 mile radius. Many attractions and prehistoric sites nearby. Art gallery with historic displays, sports centre. Trout fishing in nearby Cefni reservoir.

Ad2 Lligwy

Village near attractive sandy beach on Anglesey's east coast near Moelfre. Fascinating prehistoric burial chamber and ancient village settlement nearby.

Ac3 Malltraeth

Estuary village in south-west Anglesey, rich with wildlife. Birdwatching. Llys Llywelyn Coastal Heritage Centre at nearby Aberffraw, Glantraeth Children's Animal Park at Bodorgan.

Ad3 Menai Bridge

The first town motorists enter on Anglesey after crossing Telford's graceful Suspension Bridge (built in 1826) over the Menai Strait. Grand views of Snowdonia on mainland. Tegfryn Gallery has works by contemporary Welsh artists; Pili Palas Butterfly Farm and Anglesey Column nearby.

Aa3 Trearddur Bay

Most attractive holiday spot set amongst low cliffs on Holy Island near Holyhead. Golden sands, golf, sailing, fishing, swimming.

Trearddur Bay

Beaumaris   Bull Bay   Llangefni   Lligwy

SC | 5 Cae Morley

Llangoed, Beaumaris,
Isle of Anglesey.
LL58 8YZ
Tel: (01248) 490294

AWAITING GRADING

Near Beaumaris, bungalow sleeps 6: two double bedrooms; 1 twin bedded room; lounge with colour television; cot; high chair; fully furnished; bathroom; shower. Ample parking, quiet position, enclosed garden. Also house sleeps 4: one double bedroom; twin bedded room; colour television; fully furnished; cot; high chair; bathroom; shower. Brochure available.

P h M	🐕	PER WEEK		HOUSE	SLEEPS 6 + 4
		MIN £	MAX £	BUNGALOW	UNITS
		80.00	260.00		2
OPEN 5 - 10					

SC | Yr Orsedd

Llanddona,
Beaumaris,
Isle of Anglesey.
LL58 8TN
Tel: (01248) 810443

Traditional farmhouse close to the historic town of Beaumaris. Large lounge with exposed beams, fully fitted kitchen, very well equipped. Three bedrooms and bathroom. Large enclosed garden, barbecue area. Hilary Parry warmly welcomes you to a comfortable, luxurious, self-catering farmhouse cottage. Write or telephone for full details.

P 🍴 M	SP	PER WEEK		FARMHOUSE	SLEEPS 5 + COT
		MIN £	MAX £		UNITS
		80 .00	400.00		1
OPEN 1 - 12					

SC | Rhianfa Holiday Apartments

Bull Bay,
Amlwch,
Isle of Anglesey.
LL68 9SU
Tel: (01407) 830557

GRADE 12345

Country house apartments with lawned grounds and parking, three minutes walk down wooded lane to bay. Shops, golf, swimming pool/leisure centre 1 mile. Sleeps 2 - 6, furnished in pine, double/twin bedroom, fully equipped modern kitchen, bath or shower, colour television, games room with pool table, fitness room, laundry with washing machine, tumble dryer, cots, high chairs, cleanliness and a friendly welcome. Season/couples reductions breaks, colour brochure. Mr & Mrs T. Hill.

P h M	🐕 SP 🍴	PER WEEK		FLATS	SLEEPS 2 - 6
		MIN £	MAX £		UNITS
		80.00	260.00		7
OPEN 3 - 12					

SC | Hendre Hywel

Talwrn
Llangefni,
Isle of Anglesey.
LL77 7SB
Tel: (01248) 750593

GRADE 12345

Traditional Anglesey farmhouse of great character, listed Grade 2, built in 1690. Comfortable and spacious with modern facilities. Situated in open countryside with views to the mountains. Large well stocked and private garden. Easy access to Anglesey's beautiful beaches and Snowdonia. Walking, water sports, pony trekking, all nearby.

P h	🐕 🍴	PER WEEK		HOUSE	SLEEPS 6
		MIN £	MAX £		UNITS
		290.00	425.00		1
OPEN 6 - 10					

SC | Minffordd Caravan Park and Holiday Cottages

Lligwy, Dulas,
Isle of Anglesey.
LL70 9HJ
Tel: (01248) 410678
Fax: (01248) 410378

  GRADE 12345

Superb detached four bedroom house with spacious conservatory, surrounded by large gardens. Also nearby, two bedroom luxury character cottage, all modern facilities in both. A short distance away our delightful small garden caravan park with Dragon Award holiday homes. Fully equipped with colour TV, fridge, etc. Parking.

P h 🍴	🐕 SP	PER WEEK		HOUSE COTTAGES	SLEEPS UP TO 9
		MIN £	MAX £		UNITS
		100.00	495.00		8
OPEN 1 - 12					

TC | Tyddyn Isaf Camping and Caravan Park

Lligwy Bay, Dulas,
Isle of Anglesey.
LL70 9PQ
Tel: (01248) 410203

Superior award winning family run park overlooking Lligwy's fine sandy beach (200 yards). Excellent toilet blocks, electric hook-ups, laundry facilities, children's play area, dogs welcome (on lead), shop, private bar, serving meals. Luxury holiday homes sleeps 6, all mains services, colour TV, (Dragon Award) "AA" 4 Pennant Award. The perfect setting for a peaceful family holiday in an area of natural outstanding beauty. Write or telephone.

🐕 📷	🍴	PER NIGHT		PITCHES	STATIC 50
		MIN £	MAX £	TOURING 25	
		7.50	11.00	M/VANS 25	OPEN
				TENTS 40	3 - 10

Malltraeth   Menai Bridge   Trearddur Bay

SC Feisdon Bach

Malltraeth, Bodorgan,
Isle of Anglesey LL62 5AH
Enquiries to: Mr R.A. Jenkins
18 Arthog Road, Hale, Altrincham,
Cheshire WA15 0NA Tel: (0161) 9803253

Comfortable, secluded, fully modernised
detached, traditional Welsh cottage situated half
a mile from the picturesque and quiet coastal
village of Malltraeth on the south west coast.
Comprises two bedrooms, dining room, lounge,
kitchen bathroom/wc, cooker, microwave,
refrigerator, immersion heater, colour TV. Most
suitable for family holidays. Ideal area for bird
watching, fishing, golf, walking, pony trekking.
Fine choice of sandy beaches available within a
few miles for picnics, swimming and surfing.
Pets allowed by arrangement.

P h M	SP	PER WEEK		SLEEPS 4/5
		MIN £	MAX £	
		100.00	300.00	COTTAGE
				UNITS
OPEN 1 - 12				1

SC Plas Darien and Cliff Cottages

The Cliff,
Trearddur Bay,
Isle of Anglesey
LL65 2UR
Tel: (01407) 860789
Fax: (01407) 861150

All year round holidays and short breaks in choice
of modern centrally heated apartments with
wonderful sea views or stone built pine furnished
cottages in village-like situation very near sea.
Own private indoor leisure complex with adults
pool, sauna, solarium, gym, snooker, bowls, table
tennis. Outdoor heated pool, tennis courts,
bowls, badminton, small golf, croquet, soft ball.
Adjacent to 18 hole golf course, horse riding,
windsurfing, canoeing, fishing. Car Parking
available. Pets welcome by arrangement.

P h M	SP	PER WEEK		HOUSE	SLEEPS 2 - 8
		MIN £	MAX £		
		115.00	650.00	FLATS	UNITS
				COTTAGES	
OPEN 1 - 12					40

SCA Menai Holiday Cottages

1 Greenfield Terrace,
Hill Street, Menai Bridge,
Isle of Anglesey
LL59 5AY
Tel: (01248) 717135
Fax: (01248) 717051

Guests return year after year to generously
equipped and peaceful houses. Choose from a
converted chapel, gamekeeper's house or
traditional farmhouses, seaside cottages or
mountain retreats. Historic sites, fishing, beaches,
bird watching, walking all close by. Pets by
arrangement. We specialise in Anglesey and
Snowdonia. Telephone for our detailed brochure.

P h SP M		PER WEEK		HOUSES FARMHOUSES	SLEEPS 2 - 20
		MIN £	MAX £	FLATS	
		100.00	1500.00	COTTAGES	UNITS
				BUNGALOWS	70
OPEN 1 - 12					

SC Plas Rhianfa Properties Ltd

Glyn Garth,
Menai Bridge,
Isle of Anglesey,
LL59 5NS
Tel: (01248) 713355
Fax: (01248) 713385

Holiday apartments in unique mansion
overlooking Snowdonia and Menai Strait, set in
1½ acres of beautiful gardens to waters edge.
Games room and hard tennis court. Ideally
situated for fishing, golfing, bird watching,
walking and all water sports. Many beautiful
beaches close by. Linen and electricity included in
price. Promotional video available on request.

P h		PER WEEK			SLEEPS 2 - 7
		MIN £	MAX £		
		80.00	450.00	FLATS	UNITS
OPEN 1 - 12					16

SC Trearddur Holiday Bungalows

Lon Isallt,
Trearddur Bay,
Holyhead,
Isle of Anglesey
LL65 2UP
Tel: (01407) 860494
Fax: (01407) 861133
Central Reservations: (01502) 500500

Good quality self catering bungalows close to
Trearddur blue flag beach. Fully equipped units.
Facilities include indoor heated swimming pool,
licensed club, tennis court, sauna, solarium,
launderette, site shop. Nearby horse riding,
fishing, golf and water sports.

P h	M	PER WEEK			SLEEPS 3 - 6
		MIN £	MAX £		
		80 .00	435.00	BUNGALOWS	UNITS
OPEN 3 - 10					50

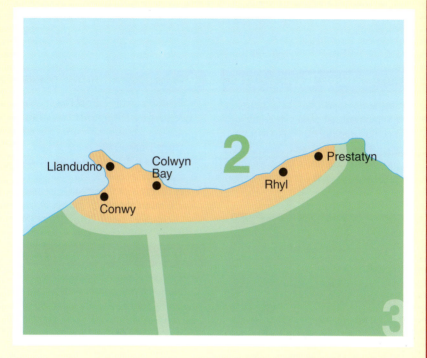

North Wales's sandy coastal strip is famous for its popular mixture of big beaches, colourful attractions and family entertainment. But within this formula there's scope for variety. Historic Conwy, with its ancient walls and castle, still retains a medieval air. Llandudno, the stately 'Queen' of the Welsh resorts, remains faithful to its Victorian roots while at the same time catering for the needs of today's visitors. For sheer seaside harmony, there's nothing quite like the view along its seafront from the headland above. Colwyn Bay, Rhyl and Prestatyn offer unpretentious fun and amusement, with huge beaches and an even larger choice of attractions, including the marvellous Welsh Mountain Zoo (Colwyn Bay), the Sun Centre (Rhyl) and the Nova Centre (Prestatyn).

It's a fact...

Llandudno's pier is over 900m/3000ft long. The resort's alpine-style Cabin Lift, one of the longest in Britain, carries passengers by cablecar for over a mile from the seafront to the summit of the Great Orme headland. Conwy has Britain's 'smallest house', a tiny fisherman's cottage on the quay. The Welsh Mountain Zoo at Colwyn Bay is owned by the Zoological Society of Wales, an educational and scientific charity. Rhyl's 73m-/240ft-high Skytower offers spectacular views from Snowdonia to Liverpool. Prestatyn is at one end of the 168-mile Offa's Dyke Path.

Bc4 Colwyn Bay

Bustling seaside resort with large sandy beach. Promenade amusements. Good touring centre for Snowdonia. Leisure centre, Eirias Park, Dinosaur World, famous Mountain Zoo with Chimpanzee World. Puppet theatre. Golf, tennis, riding and other sports. Quieter Rhos on Sea at western end of bay.

Bb3 Llandudno

Premier coastal resort of North Wales with everything the holidaymaker needs. Two beaches, spacious promenade, Victorian pier, excellent shopping. Donkey rides. Punch and Judy, ski slope. Alice in Wonderland exhibition, art gallery, museum, old copper mines open to the public, splendid North Wales Theatre. Visit the Great Orme headland above the resort and ride by cabinlift or tramway. Conference centre. Many daily excursions.

Be3 Prestatyn

Family seaside resort on popular North Wales coast. Entertainment galore at superb Nova Centre including heated swimming pools and aquashute. Sailing, swimming on long, sandy coastline. Close to pastoral Vale of Clwyd and Clwydian Range.

Colwyn Bay (top)

Llandudno's pier and promenade

SC — Bron-y-Wendon Holiday Cottages

Bron-y-Wendon,
Wern Road,
Llanddulas,
Colwyn Bay.
LL22 8HG
Tel: (01492) 512903

Our new, luxury, centrally heated cottages are part of a farmhouse conversion and offer the ultimate in self-catering accommodation. Facilities include satellite TV, dishwasher, washing machine, microwave and games room. Ideally situated for seaside or touring. All cottages have sea views and the beach is approx 300 yds away. Llanddulas is a small village with shops and good pubs. Facilities nearby include leisure complex, horse riding and golf. Short breaks all year. Colour brochure available.

P	h	PER WEEK			SLEEPS
h	SP	MIN £	MAX £	COTTAGES	2 - 5 + BABY
		150.00	357.00		UNITS
		OPEN 1 - 12			5

SC — The Olde Granary

Maerdy Mawr, Gwyddelwern,
Corwen. LL21 9SD
Enquiries To: Green Gates,
Abergele Road, St Asaph, LL17 OLE
Tel: (01745) 583201

One and two bedroom cottages, pleasantly converted granary and farm buildings on 250 acre sheep farm 1/2 mile Gwyddelwern (shop and pub) between Corwen and medieval town Ruthin. Bala and Llangollen 13 miles. All with beamed sitting rooms, kitchen/diner, bath/shower rooms. Views over fields to Berwyn range. Excellent base for exploring and touring all North Wales. Golf, sailing, swimming, tennis, fishing, horse riding within 13 miles.

P	h	PER WEEK			SLEEPS
M		MIN £	MAX £	COTTAGES	2 - 6
		120.00	200.00	BUNGALOWS	UNITS
		OPEN 1 - 12			4

SC — Augusta Holiday Flats

7 Augusta Street,
Llandudno.
LL30 2AE
Tel: (01492) 878330

Near sea, central shopping, trains and coach stations, theatre and all resort facilities. On level ground, no front steps. 40 completely self contained apartments, various sizes, some ground floor. Each with private bathroom, toilet, colour television, well equipped kitchen, full size refrigerator, forecourt parking, economy tariff electricity. Resident manageress. Colour brochure. 24 hour telephone.

P	h	PER WEEK			SLEEPS
SP	M	MIN £	MAX £	FLATS	2 - 8
		99.00	299.00		UNITS
		OPEN 1 - 12			40

SC — Buile Hill Holiday Flats

46 St Marys Road
Llandudno
LL30 2UE
Tel: (01492) 876972

Centrally situated, quiet select area. Within easy walking distance of shops, theatre, coach, railway terminals. Flats fully self-contained. Equipped with full size cookers, microwaves, fridge, colour TV. Cleanliness assured. Open all year. Special prices for out of season bookings.

P	h	PER WEEK			SLEEPS
h	SP	MIN £	MAX £	FLATS	2 - 4
		105.00	250.00		UNITS
		OPEN 1 - 12			6

SC — The Gogarth Abbey Hotel Apartments

West Shore
Llandudno.
LL30 2QY
Tel: (01492) 876211
Fax: (01492) 875805
Central Res: Freephone 0500 400 472

Within the Gogarth Abbey Hotel we offer 3 luxury self catering apartments, each one fully equipped and enjoying a superb setting with magnificent views. Enjoy the freedom of self-catering and the facilities of one of Llandudno's best hotels all in one. Open all year.

P	h	PER WEEK			SLEEPS
h	SP	MIN £	MAX £	FLATS	3 - 6
		250.00	500.00		UNITS
		OPEN 1 - 12			3

TC — Penrhyn Hall Farm Caravan Park

Penrhyn Bay,
Llandudno.
LL30 3EE
Tel: (01492) 549207

Beaches, museums, mines, ski slope, toboggan run, golf courses, pony trekking, leisure centre, theatre, castle, cruises, shopping centres within 5 miles. Each touring site has a concrete standing, tap, drain, free electrical hook-up point. Playground, payphone, laundrette with ironing facilities, elsan point. Dish washing area, clean toilet and shower block, hair and hand dryer.

		PER NIGHT		PITCHES	STATIC
		MIN £	MAX £	TOURING 8	151
		9.00	10.50	M/VANS 2	OPEN
					4 - 10

CP — Lido Beach Holiday Park

Central Beach,
Bastion Road,
Prestatyn LL19 7EU
Tel: (0345) 697116
Fax: (01745) 887123
Central Reservations: (0345) 508508

Lido Beach is a Welsh Holidays Park, found in a peaceful setting with direct access to a vast sandy beach. The fabulous Nova Centre is just a short walk away, offers excellent entertainment and facilities. For a free brochure call (0345) 697116 or contact your local travel agent.

		PER WEEK		No. OF CARAVANS	
		MIN £	MAX £	STATIC	HIRING
		99.00	409.00	689	50
				OPEN 3 - 11	

Wales's border country is a mix of rolling green hills, lovely valleys, high moor and forest. The airy Clwydian Range guards the broad and fertile Vale of Clwyd – one of Wales's richest farming areas – which is dotted with historic towns. The valley around Llangollen is much deeper, its steep-sided hills rising to dramatic heights with names like 'World's End'. The wild moorlands above Denbigh are covered in heather and forest – and the waters of Llyn Brenig, a huge reservoir with many leisure facilities. There's much to see and do in this exhilarating area – walking, riding, canal cruising, and visiting places like Bodelwyddan Castle, where paintings from the National Portrait Gallery are exhibited, and Erddig, Wrexham, an unusual 'upstairs, downstairs' country house owned by the National Trust.

It's a fact...

The Clwydian Range of hills on the eastern flank of the Vale of Clwyd were designated an 'Area of Outstanding Natural Beauty' in 1985. Their summit, Moel Fammau, stands at 555m/1821ft. St Asaph has Britain's smallest cathedral. Llangollen's famous International Musical Eisteddfod was first held in 1947 to help bring countries together after war. Ruthin's medieval credentials are reinforced by the custom of the curfew bell, which is still rung at 8pm each night. Sir Henry Morton Stanley, who found Dr Livingstone in Africa, was born in Denbigh.

Be7   Corwen

Pleasant market town in Vale of Edeyrnion. Livestock market held regularly. Fishing in River Dee, swimming pool, good walks. Well-located touring centre for Snowdonia and border country.

Ec1   Llangollen

Romantic town on River Dee, famous for its International Musical Eisteddfod; singers and dancers from all over the world come here every July. The town's many attractions include a canal museum, pottery, weavers, ECTARC European Centre for Traditional and Regional Cultures and a standard-gauge steam railway. Plas Newydd (home of 'Ladies of Llangollen' fame) is nearby. Valle Crucis Abbey is 2 miles away in a superb setting and ruined Castell Dinas Brân overlooks the town. Browse through the town's little shops; stand on its 14th-century stone bridge; cruise along the canal. Golf course and wonderful walking in surrounding countryside.

Eb3   Llanrhaeadr ym Mochnant

Pastoral calm befits the village where Bishop William Morgan translated the Bible into Welsh in the 1580s. Best known today for its proximity to highest waterfall in Wales, Pistyll Rhaeadr (73m/240ft), one of the 'Seven Wonders of Wales'. Popular spot for walking and pony trekking.

Ca6   Ruthin

Attractive and historic market town noted for its fine architecture; curfew is still rung nightly. Many captivating old buildings. Medieval banquets in Ruthin Castle. Ancient St Peter's Church has beautiful gates and carved panels. Good range of small shops; craft centre with workshops. Ideal base for Vale of Clwyd.

Cc6   Wrexham

Busy industrial and commercial town, gateway to North Wales. St Giles's Church has graceful tower and altar piece given by Elihu Yale of Yale University fame (his tomb is in the churchyard). Visit Erddig Hall, an unusual country house on outskirts, and the Clywedog Valley Heritage Park. Good shopping and excellent little heritage centre. Industrial museum at neighbouring Bersham. Art gallery, swimming pool, golf.

Ruthin (top)

Llangollen

Llangollen   Ruthin   Wrexham

Pistyll Rhaeadr waterfall

SC | Groeslwyd

Rhewl,
Llangollen. LL20 7AJ

Enquiries to: Mrs G. Roberts
7 Thornhurst Ave, Oswestry,
Shropshire. SY11 1NR
Tel: (01691) 655179

17th century farmhouse, oak beamed with inglenook, on the banks of the Dee commanding panoramic views over the Vale of Llangollen. It is set in ten acres of field and woodland with riverside frontage. An area of special scientific interest, it is also an ideal base for touring North Wales.

P h		PER WEEK		SLEEPS 5 - 6
M		MIN £	MAX £	
		200.00	275.00	COTTAGE
		OPEN 4 - 10		UNITS 1

SC | Tyddyn Isaf

Rhewl,
Ruthin LL15 1UH
Enquiries to: Mrs E. Jones
Cerrig, Fford Gwynach,
Ruthin LL15 1DE
Tel: (01824) 703142 or 703367

A warm welcome awaits you on this 80 acre working farm, with spacious accommodation in self-contained part of farmhouse and in a recently converted granary. Both fully equipped. Splendid views of the Clwydian hills, 3 miles from Ruthin. Convenient for visiting Chester, Llangollen, Betws-y- Coed. Garden patio sets, central heating winter months, bed linen inclusive. Sorry no pets.

P h		PER WEEK		SLEEPS 2 - 6
SP M		MIN £	MAX £	
		90.00	240.00	FARMHOUSES
		OPEN 1 - 12		UNITS 2

SCA | Alyn Cottages

Stoneleigh,
Willow Court,
Bangor-on-Dee,
Wrexham LL13 OBT
Tel: (01978) 780679
Fax/Tel: (01978) 780770

AWAITING GRADING

Cottages and other properties situated in and around the Welsh Borderlands/North Wales. Fully equipped providing comfort and peace. Attractions include National Trust properties, steam railways and craft shops. Activities include paragliding, canoeing, walking, fishing, riding, golfing, plus many others. Discount vouchers to visit attractions given with each booking. Write or telephone for information.

P		PER WEEK		HOUSES	SLEEPS 2 - 8
h		MIN £	MAX £	FARMHOUSES	
SP		60.00	550.00	COTTAGES	
		OPEN 1 - 12		BUNGALOWS	UNITS 12+

This part of Wales takes its name from the jagged pinnacle of Snowdon. Yet the Snowdonia National Park extends southwards for hundreds of square miles from Snowdon itself, all the way to Dolgellau and beyond, and eastwards to Bala. All of Wales's high and mighty mountains are here – Tryfan, the Glyders, the Carneddau, the Aran and Arennigs, and Cader Idris. Snowdonia, a place of surprising scenic variety, also has its oakwood vales, its forested hills, its lakes and rivers, its brooding moorlands. Mountains sweep down to the sea along a beautiful coastline of sandy beaches and estuaries. And along the Llŷn Peninsula – 'Snowdonia's arm' – you'll find some of the wildest coastal scenery in Britain as well as sheltered beaches and picturesque little resorts.

It's a fact...

The Snowdonia National Park covers 838 square miles. It was Wales's first national park, designated in 1951. Snowdonia's Welsh name is *Eryri*, which means 'the mountain of the eagles'. The peak of Snowdon stands at 1085m/3560ft, the highest mountain in England and Wales. The Llŷn Peninsula has the highest percentage of Welsh speakers in Wales (75%). Llŷn was declared an 'Area of Outstanding Natural Beauty' in 1956. Bwlch y Groes, the mountain road between Dinas Mawddwy and Bala, is Wales's highest road, climbing to 546m/1791ft. Bala Lake is Wales's largest natural lake.

Db6 Aberdovey/Aberdyfi

Picturesque little resort and dinghy sailor's paradise on the Dovey Estuary. All watersports, thriving yacht club, good inns looking out over the bay and 18-hole golf links. Superb views towards hills and mountains.

Ac5 Abersoch

Dinghy sailing and windsurfing centre with sandy beaches. Superb coastal scenery with easy walks. Pony trekking, golf, fishing and sea trips. Llanengan's historic church nearby.

De2 Bala

Traditional Welsh country town with tree-lined main street and interesting little shops. Narrow-gauge railway runs one side of Bala Lake, 4 miles long (the largest natural lake in Wales) and ringed with mountains. Golf, sailing, fishing, canoeing – a natural touring centre for Snowdonia.

Ae3 Bangor

Compact cathedral city of character overlooking the Menai Strait; gateway to Anglesey and Snowdonia's Ogwen Valley, with university college and 6th-century cathedral. Attractions include Theatr Gwynedd, Penrhyn Castle, museum and art gallery and an exquisitely renovated pier. Heated swimming pool, yachting and fishing.

Db4 Barmouth

Superbly located resort at the mouth of lovely Mawddach Estuary. Golden sands, miles of wonderful mountain and estuary walks nearby. Promenade, funfair, harbour and pony rides on the beach. Lifeboat and Shipwreck Centre museums. Good shops and inns. Excellent parking on seafront.

Ae6 Beddgelert

Village romantically set amid glorious mountain scenery, with Nant Gwynant Valley to the east and rocky Aberglaslyn Pass to the south. Snowdonia's grandeur all around; Wordsworth made a famous dawn ascent of Mount Snowdon from here. Marvellous walks; links with legendary dog named Gelert. Visit Sygun Copper Mine and Cae Du Farm Park, two nearby attractions.

Bb6 Betws-y-Coed

Wooded village and popular mountain resort in picturesque setting where three rivers meet. Good touring centre, close to best mountain area of Snowdonia. Tumbling rivers and waterfalls emerge from a tangle of treetops. Trout fishing, craft shops, golf course, railway and motor museums, Snowdonia National Park Visitor Centre. Nature trails very popular with hikers. Swallow Falls a 'must'.

Ba7 Blaenau Ffestiniog

One-time centre of the Welsh slate industry, now a tourist town with two cavernous slate quarries – Llechwedd and Gloddfa Ganol – open to visitors. Narrow-gauge Ffestiniog Railway runs from Porthmadog. Nearby Stwlan Dam, part of hydro-electric scheme, reached through marvellous mountain scenery. Visitor centre explains how electricity is generated.

Ad4 Caernarfon

Dominated by magnificent 13th-century castle, most famous of Wales's medieval fortresses. Many museums in castle, maritime museum in town. Caernarfon Air World at Dinas Dinlle, Segontium Roman Fort and Museum on hill above town. Popular sailing centre, old harbour, market square, Lloyd George statue. Holiday centre at gateway of Snowdonia. Parc Glynllifon nearby.

Ad7 Criccieth

Ideal family resort with good beach. Romantic ruined castle on headland overlooking sea. Salmon and trout in nearby rivers and lakes. Festival of Music and the Arts in June. Village of Llanystumdwy with Lloyd George Museum nearby.

Ad6 Garndolbenmaen

Small hillside village high above the sea, 4 miles from Criccieth. Nearby woollen mill to visit and excellent walking. Good base for touring Llŷn Peninsula and Snowdonia.

Dc4 Dolgellau

Handsome stone-built market town which seems to have grown naturally out of the mountains. The heights of Cader Idris loom above the rooftops. Interesting shops, pubs, cafes. Museum of the Quakers in town centre. Visit a gold mine in nearby forest. Excellent base for touring the coast and countryside.

Da3 Llanbedr

Llanbedr and neighbouring Pensarn form a duo of attractive villages on the Ardudwy coast near Harlech. Maes Artro Village a popular family tourist attraction. Close to Shell Island at Mochras, and slate caverns. The wild Rhinog Mountains in the background are excellent for walking. Explore them from lovely Llyn Cwm Bychan.

Bb6 Dolwyddelan

Village on A470 at the foot of Moel Siabod in the Snowdonia National Park. Convenient for exploring Gwydyr Forest and North Wales coast resorts. Excellent walking countryside. Imposing 13th-century stone castle, stronghold of Llywelyn the Great, Prince of Wales. 12th-century church.

Ab7 Llanbedrog

Small resort with sheltered sands, popular with families. Wooded walls, Mynydd Tir y Cwmwd headland with spectacular views across Tremadog Bay. Visit Plas Glyn-y-Weddw, a fascinating historic house and art gallery. Well located within easy reach of Pwllheli and Abersoch.

Da3 Dyffryn Ardudwy

Pleasant village near the coast on Barmouth–Harlech road, set between sea and mountains. Prehistoric burial chamber and stone circles nearby; also scenic Shell Island and Museum of Transport.

The narrow-guage Ffestiniog Railway

Caernarfon Castle (top)

Bb6   Llanrwst

Attractive town where the crystal-clear River Conwy runs through lush meadows; chief shopping centre of upper Conwy Valley. Handsome bridge designed by Inigo Jones in 1636. Gwydir Park has bowling, putting and children's playground. Charming Gwydir Uchaf Chapel and scenic Llyn Geirionydd in woodlands above town. Gwydir Castle open to the public. Bodnant Garden 8 miles away.

Ab6   Morfa Nefyn

Popular north Llŷn seaside village, with extensive sandy beaches, between little harbour of Porthdinllaen and resort of Nefyn. Set against mountainous backdrop of Garn Boduan. Historical and Maritime Museum at Nefyn.

Ab6   Nefyn

Old fishing village on north coast of Llŷn Peninsula perched above sweeping bay. 2 miles of sand, swimming, sailing and fishing. Visit the Llŷn Historical and Maritime Museum.

Ae7   Porthmadog

Harbour town and shopping centre named after William Madocks, who built mile-long Cob embankment. Steam narrow-gauge Ffestiniog Railway runs to Blaenau Ffestiniog, with its slate caverns. Also Welsh Highland Railway. Pottery, maritime museum, car museum. Portmeirion Italianate village and good beaches nearby.

Ac7   Pwllheli

A small resort big in appeal to sailors; many craft are moored in its attractive marina. Promenade with excellent spacious beach, shopping, golf, leisure centre. River and sea fishing. Exciting Starcoast World, a major North Wales attraction, nearby.

Da6   Tywyn

Seaside resort on Cardigan Bay, with beach activities, sea and river fishing and golf among its leading attractions. Good leisure centre. Narrow-gauge Talyllyn Railway runs inland from here and St Cadfan's Stone and Llanegryn Church are important Christian monuments. In the hills stand Castell-y-Bere, a native Welsh castle, and Bird Rock, a haven for birdlife.

Llyn Gwynant, Snowdonia

SC | Aberdovey Hillside Village

Church Street,
Aberdovey
LL35 0ND
Tel: (01654) 767522
Fax: (01654) 767069

Quality self-catering on the mid Wales coast. A small cluster of architect designed cottages, houses and apartments with stunning views of the Dovey estuary. 250 yards from sandy beach, restaurants and village amenities. All units have south facing balconies or terraces. Central facilities include fitness room, table tennis, pool table and satellite television.

		PER WEEK			SLEEPS
P			HOUSES		2 - 8
h	SP	MIN £	MAX £	FLATS	
		100.00	695.00	COTTAGES	UNITS
		OPEN 1 - 12			22

SC | Abersoch Riding Centre

Tyddyn Talgoch Uchaf,
Bwlchtocyn,
Nr Abersoch
LL53 7BT
Tel: (01758) 712285
Fax: (01758) 712285

In an Area of Outstanding Natural Beauty, a spacious farmhouse (sleeps 10) with spectacular views of Cardigan Bay and Snowdonia. Within walking distance of two superb beaches and many more within easy reach. Watersports, fishing, boat trips, golf, clay pigeon shooting and archery nearby. All riding activities available at adjacent riding centre.

		PER WEEK			SLEEPS
P			FARMHOUSE		2 - 10
h	SP	MIN £	MAX £	FLAT	
M		50.00	500.00	CAMPUS	UNITS
		OPEN 1 - 12		ACCOMMODATION	2

SC | Pen-y-Benar

Abersoch
LL53 7AY
Tel: (01758) 712984

Set in beautiful gardens 200 yards from the sandy beach and yacht club. A short walk to the shops and golf course. Ample room to park your car by your own front door. Out of season breaks a speciality. Open all year.

		PER WEEK			SLEEPS
P	h				4 AND 6
SP	M	MIN £	MAX £	FLATS	
		135.00	425.00	COTTAGES	UNITS
		OPEN 1 - 12			3

SC | Tai Gwyliau Tŷ'n Don Holiday Cottages

Llanengan,
Pwllheli, LL53 7LG
Enquiries to: Mrs Evans,
Penlan, Rhos Isaf,
Caernarfon, LL54 7NG
Tel: (01286) 831184

2 miles from Abersoch. Peaceful, relaxing stone cottages. 300 yards and overlooking Porth Neigwl (Hell's Mouth) beach with private access. Fully equipped. personal supervision. Launderette, payphone, children's play area. Short breaks. Brochure.

		PER WEEK			SLEEPS
P					5 - 8
h	SP	MIN £	MAX £	FARMHOUSE	
M		99.00	390.00	COTTAGES	UNITS
		OPEN 1 - 12			11

SC | Y Bwythyn

c/o Tŷ Capel,
Llwyn Einion,
Bala
LL23 7PN
Enquiries to: Mrs B. Davies
Tel: (01678) 520572

Situated in a quiet position in Snowdonia National Park, overlooking Arenig mountain. Two bedrooms, one double, two singles. Modern kitchen, storage heaters. Good centre for visiting sea and mountains. Walking, fishing, sailing, canoeing, pony trekking, golf. Bala 3 miles. Enquiries to Mrs B. Davies.

		PER WEEK			SLEEPS
h	M				4
		MIN £	MAX £	COTTAGE	
		75.00	100.00		UNITS
		OPEN 4 - 10			1

SC | Hen Hafod and Fedw'r Gog

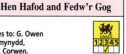

Nr Bala
Enquiries to: G. Owen
Penisarmynydd,
Maerdy, Corwen.
Tel: (01490) 460448

These are ideal, peaceful, private locations for the country lover. The properties are surrounded by beautiful countryside with a wealth of wildlife. Situated on sheep farms, at the end of a concrete road and within easy reach of the market town of Bala, in the Snowdonia National Park. Stone built cottages of charm and character, exposed beams, inglenook fireplace. All modern amenities. Bed linen provided. Ideal for touring North Wales. Pets welcome.

		PER WEEK			SLEEPS
P					2 - 7
h	SP	MIN £	MAX £	FARMHOUSE	
M		100.00	240.00	COTTAGE	UNITS
		OPEN 1 - 12			3

SC | Plas Madog

Parc,
Bala, LL23 7YN
Enquiries to: E.T. and M.W. Pugh
Glanllyn,
Llanuwchllyn,
Bala, LL23 7ST
Tel: (01678) 540227

Situated in beautiful countryside with a large enclosed garden. Private access for fishing, launching boats, windsurfing and canoeing on Bala lake. Large oak kitchen, dining room, lounge with satellite TV, cellar with snooker table, games and satellite TV, four bedrooms. Two bathrooms, laundry. Idyllic for a peaceful holiday.

		PER WEEK			SLEEPS
P	h				6 + 2
SP		MIN £	MAX £	FARMHOUSE	
		200.00	400.00		UNITS
		OPEN 1 - 12			1

Bala   Bangor   Barmouth

SC | Tyddyn Du

Parc,
Bala
LL23 7YS
Tel: (01678) 540244

Modernised comfortable accommodation. Colour television, microwave, fridge freezer, utility room facilities. Ideal centre for North Wales. Patio, conservatory, enclosed garden, panoramic views. Country walks, leisure centre, pony trekking within six miles. Seaside resorts thirty miles. First five pounds electricity and heating included. Ample parking space. Ideal for families or those interested in a quiet retreat.

P h SP		PER WEEK		SLEEPS 6
		MIN £ 150.00	MAX £ 245.00	FARMHOUSE	UNITS 1
		OPEN 1 - 12		

SC | Fodol Newydd

Hafod Lane,
Bangor
LL57 4BU
Tel: (01248) 670305

Modern, spacious, self-contained farmhouse on a family run dairy farm, in country area outside Bangor. Ideal base for touring Snowdonia, Anglesey and Llŷn Peninsula. Panoramic views over the mountain ranges. All linen and household essentials provided. Safe lawned garden, patio and verandah. Children welcome. No pets. Ample parking. Shops five minutes away. Croeso.

P M	PER WEEK		SLEEPS 6
	MIN £ 95.00	MAX £ 210.00	FARMHOUSE	UNITS 1
	OPEN 1 - 12		

SC | Plas Caerdeon

Plas Caerdeon Outdoor Education Centre,
Bontddu,
Barmouth, LL42 1TH
Tel: (01341) 430276
Fax: (01341) 430276

Plas Caerdeon, set in 18 acres of wooded grounds, overlooks the beautiful Mawddach estuary. This imposing Victorian mansion, 300 metres from the Dolgellau to Barmouth road, has two self-contained cottages in a converted stables block. The surrounding area is ideal for a variety of holiday activities. Mountain moorland, woodland and the coast are within easy reach. Heating by NSH. Ample parking. TV and all normal domestic services. Open throughout the year.

P h SP	PER WEEK		SLEEPS 6
	MIN £ 195.00	MAX £ 280.00	COTTAGES	UNITS 2
	OPEN 1 - 12		

SC | Talarfor

Llanaber,
Barmouth
LL42 1BQ
Enquiries to: J. Clark
Tel: (01341) 280069

Quietly situated 1 mile from a typical seaside town. Self-contained ground floor flat, with patio, overlooking superb sandy beach and garden. A 2 minute walk to beach. Parking. 2 bedrooms, linen provided. Resident proprietor ensures high standards and friendly welcome.

P h	PER WEEK		SLEEPS 5 + COT
SP	MIN £ 85.00	MAX £ 240.00	FLAT	UNITS 1
	OPEN 1 - 12		

CP | Hendre Coed Isaf Caravan Park

Llanaber,
Barmouth
LL42 1AJ
Tel: (01341) 280597
Fax: (01341) 280442

A peaceful, friendly, family run park. Hillside location within the Snowdonia National Park. Terraced caravans with superb views of picturesque Cardigan Bay. Dragon Award caravans. Pet/pet-free. Olde worlde club, bar meals and take-away. Games room, shop, launderette. Outdoor swimming pool. Golf, fishing, pony trekking, etc. All nearby.

	PER WEEK		No. OF CARAVANS	
			STATIC 93	HIRING 22
	MIN £ 95.00	MAX £ 325.00		
			OPEN 4 - 10	

CP | Parc Caerelwan

Talybont,
Barmouth
LL43 2AX
Tel: (01341) 247236
Fax: (01341) 247711

Quiet family run holiday park offering top quality caravan-bungalows and caravans at affordable prices. Picturesque beach mountain location. Sauna, steam room, solarium, fitness suite, launderette, shop, table-tennis, crazy golf, tots fun room, pool tables. Sailing and pony trekking nearby. Ideal base for exploring Snowdonia. Pets welcome.

	SP	PER WEEK		No. OF CARAVANS	
				STATIC 150	HIRING 95
		MIN £ 80.00	MAX £ 310.00		
				OPEN 1 - 12	

Bala Lake

SC | Cae Dafydd Farm

Llanfrothen
LL48 6SN
Tel: (01766) 890474
Fax: (01766) 771396

Comfortable self-contained apartment in historic farmhouse set in beautiful Nantmor Valley, Snowdonia. Ideally situated for touring, walking, sea, mountains. Family-run farm with wide range of animals. Generously equipped, the apartment has three bedrooms, shower room, farmhouse kitchen/living room with all amenities. Colour TV, laundry room. All linen provided. Heated throughout. Own garden with barbecue. Off season mini breaks. Regrettably no pets. Children welcome, cot, high chair, baby-sitting facilities.

		PER WEEK			SLEEPS
P	h	MIN £	MAX £	FARMHOUSE	6
SP	M	120.00	290.00		UNITS
		OPEN 1 - 12			1

SC | Colwyn

Beddgelert
LL55 4UJ
Tel: (01766) 890276

Two old stone cottages in the centre of a picturesque and unspoiled village right at the foot of Snowdon. Surrounded by mountains, forests, lakes and streams. Maxi cottage, overlooking the river-bridge, sleeps 6/8. Mini upside-down cottage 100 yds away, sleeps 2. Fully carpeted, furnished and equipped including white linen towels, elec blankets. All bedrooms en-suite. C. htg. Village inns, shops and good food all within 100 yds. Elec. at standard rate, parking adjacent, no garden. Walkers, muddy boots and wet dogs welcome. Unsuitable for small children or the infirm. Please call me or my tame Ansafone, for bookings or info. 01766 890276.

THREE EN-SUITE BEDROOMS SLEEP 6:	PER WEEK £390.00
FOUR EN-SUITE BEDROOMS SLEEP 8:	PER WEEK £480.00
MINI-COTTAGE (MAR-OCT) SLEEP 2:	PER WEEK £160.00
MAXI WINTER W/END OR M/WK 3 NTS: 6/£180.00 8/£240.00	

SC | Glan-y-Borth Holiday Village

Betws Road
Llanrwst
LL26 0HE
Tel: (01492) 641543
Fax: (01492) 641369

Glan-y-Borth nestles peacefully on the banks of the river Conwy. Fully equipped bungalows with home from home comfort. Six bungalows designed for wheelchairs. Magnificent scenery with an abundance of attractions and activities, mountain railways, walking, canoeing, castles and sandy beaches. Please contact Bill between 8.00am and 9.00pm daily.

		PER WEEK			SLEEPS
P	h	MIN £	MAX £	FLATS	2 - 8
h		80 .00	330.00	BUNGALOWS	
	M			CHALETS	UNITS
SP		OPEN 1 - 12			21

SC | Waterloo Hotel

Betws-y-Coed
LL24 0AR
Tel: (01690) 710411
Fax: (01690) 710666

The leading hotel in Snowdonia with hotel and motel rooms. Ideal location for touring mountains and the beautiful coastlines. The newly built self-catering cottages have en-suites, colour TV, telephone, tea/coffe trays, hairdryer. All bedding and power supplied. Hotel facilities - garden room restaurant, choice of bars, coffee shop. Indoor leisure complex swimming pool, jacuzzi, steam room, sauna, solarium, mutigym. Slate mines, castles, pony treking, main tourist attractions in this choice vicinity.

		PER WEEK			SLEEPS
P	h	MIN £	MAX £	COTTAGES	5
		355.00	460.00		UNITS
		OPEN 1 - 12			4

SC | Offeren Cottage

1 Cwmbowydd Lane,
Blaenau Ffestiniog, LL41 3EE
Enquiries to: Mr & Mrs E.H. Preston,
3 Banks Mount,
Pontrefact, Yorkshire, WF8 4DN
Tel: (01977) 703092
Central Reservations: (01766) 830982

Fully equipped cottage with three bedrooms, bathroom and separate shower room, dining room, kitchen and lounge with open fire, colour TV and piano. Extra cot/small child's bed. Near shops and restaurants. Ideal for family, touring, walking or climbing holidays. Automatic washing machine. Indoor drying. Beaches, riding, fly-fishing, steam trains near. Small garden.

		PER WEEK			SLEEPS
P	h	MIN £	MAX £	COTTAGE	6
h	SP	75.00	250.00		UNITS
		OPEN 1 - 12			1

SC | Bron Rhiw

Lon-y-Buarth,
Carmel,
Nr Caernarfon, LL54 7RB
Tel: (01286) 880069
Fax: (01286) 880069

Detached self-contained 18th century stone cottage maintained to high standards. Includes satellite TV, dishwasher, telephone microwave, central heating. Set within 2 acre smallholding. Peaceful countryside. Nearest village 1/2 mile. Elevated position giving stupendous panoramic views of Anglesey, Caernarfon and bays. Caernarfon and beaches 6 miles. Ideal for Snowdonia. Winter breaks. Traditional curry and Balti dishes available.

		PER WEEK			SLEEPS
P	h	MIN £	MAX £	COTTAGE	2
SP	M	125.00	200.00		UNITS
		OPEN 1 - 12			1

Caernarfon

SC Bryn Bras Castle

Llanrug, Nr Caernarfon
LL55 4RE
Tel: (01286) 870210
Fax: (01286) 870210

Welcome to beautiful Bryn Bras Castle - romantic apartments, elegant tower house, mini-cottage within distinctive Romanesque castle, enjoying breathtaking scenery amid gentle Snowdonia foothills. Easy reach mountains, beaches, heritage, local restaurants/inns. Each fully self-contained, individual character, spacious, peaceful. Maid service available. Generously equipped from dishwasher .... flowers. Central heating, hot water, linen - free. All highest grade (ex. one). 32 acre gardens, woodlands, panoramic walks. Warmth, convenience, comfort in serene surroundings. Short breaks all year from £95.00.

P h SP M ☎	PER WEEK	TOWER HOUSE CASTLE APARTS MINI COTTAGE	SLEEPS 2 - 4
	MIN £	MAX £	
	170.00	510.00	UNITS
	OPEN 1 - 12		8

SC Executive Beach Bungalow

West Point,
The Beach, Pontllyfni,
Caernarfon, LL54 5ET
Tel: (01286) 660400

In an area of outstanding natural beauty. A quiet secluded cove, your own beach moments from your lounge patio door. Modern split level lounge dining room. Every comfort, 1-4 bedrooms, 2 bathrooms, teletext TV, video, CD music centre, dishwasher, microwave, fridge, freezer, washer tumble dryer, phone, electric blankets, central heating 70°. Parking 5 cars. Boating, bathing, fishing, walking on flat coastal strip. Golf, restaurants nearby, bar snacks, PO shop, tour Snowdonia. Featured by BBC. View anytime. Try a £49 minibreak now. Phone for brochure.

P ⌂ h SP ☎	PER WEEK	BUNGALOW	SLEEPS 10
	MIN £	MAX £	
	89.00	549.00	UNITS
	OPEN 1 - 12		1

SC Hafoty

Rhostryfan
Caernarfon
LL54 7PH
Tel: (01286) 830144

WTB Tourism Award. Two small cottages lovingly restored from old mill and stable. Situated in beautiful Snowdonia, overlooking Caernarfon Castle and Anglesey. Fully equipped to high standard. Your very own patio with picnic table and barbecue. The cottages form part of the courtyard at Hafoty's Farm Licensed Guest House.

P h SP M ☎	PER WEEK	COTTAGES	SLEEPS 2 + BABY
	MIN £	MAX £	
	100.00	250.00	UNITS
	OPEN 1 - 12		2

SC Bryn-y-Maen

Llanrug,
Caernarfon
LL55 4RY
Enquiries to: Mrs Ellis Owen
Tel: (01286) 870090

Well appointed country cottage, owner supervised on residential small farm at foothills of Snowdonia. Peacefully located, it commands panoramic views. Ideal touring base for mountains and beaches of peninsula and Anglesey. All modern amenities. Welsh antiques adding character and homely atmosphere. Lounge/diner, fully equipped kitchen, two double bedrooms and bathroom. Attractive grounds, ample parking. Telephone/SAE for brochure.

P ⌂ h SP M	PER WEEK	COTTAGE	SLEEPS 4/5 MAX
	MIN £	MAX £	
	150.00	220.00	UNITS
	OPEN 3 - 10		1

SC Glyn Gwynedd (The Old Bakery)

Rhostryfan
Caernarfon
LL54 7PD
Tel: (01286) 881022

Charming cottage tucked away in peaceful village, between mountains and sea. Free electricity, central heating, all linen, towels, total comfort, log fires, TVs, video, barbecue, pretty garden, stream safely fenced. Perfect family centre for all attractions, Snowdonia, Anglesey. Polite pets welcomed. Discount for couples. Short breaks. Illustrated brochure.

P ⌂ h SP ☎	PER WEEK	COTTAGE	SLEEPS 6 + COT
	MIN £	MAX £	
	230.00	390.00	UNITS
	OPEN 1 - 12		1

CP Beach Holiday West Point

The Beach,
Pontllyfni
Caernarfon
LL54 5ET
Tel: (01286) 660400

Welcome to our world by the sea. Beach villa chalet, new super 12ft wide caravans. Your own beach moments from patio door, quiet seclusion, every comfort, luxury lounge overlooking lawn, beach & sea, lounge suite, dining room table and chairs, 1, 2 or 3 bedrooms, bathroom, teletext colour TV, microwave, electric blankets and bedroom heater. Free electric and gas. Well heated to 70°. Adjacent parking, boating, fishing, bathing, nearby restaurants, bar snacks. Featured by BBC and WTB, view anytime. Try a £12 mini break now. Brochure.

⌂ SP ⌷ 👤	No. OF CARAVANS	
	STATIC	HIRING
	50	50
MIN £	MAX £	
79.00	339.00	
OPEN 3 - 10		

Caernarfon

CP | Bryn Gloch Caravan & Camping Park

Betws Garmon,
Caernarfon,
LL54 7YY
Tel: (01286) 650216
Fax: (01286) 650216

One of the most picturesque sites in Wales overlooked by the Snowdonia Mountain Ranges on bank of River Gwyrfai in Vale of Betws. Mount Snowdon only 2 miles. Ancient town of Caernarfon 5 miles, Isle of Anglesey and Llŷn Peninsula 30 minutes drive. As a local family we insist that the site is kept clean and quiet and have received the Dragon Award from the WTB. Within 15 minute drive pony trekking, beach boating and canoeing. 30 minutes dry ski slope and paragliding. SAE for brochure.

🐕 🍴	WEEKLY RATES		No. OF CARAVANS	
SP ⊡			STATIC	HIRING
✕ 🍺	MIN £	MAX £	15	13
⌂	105.00	250.00	OPEN 3 - 11	

CP | Plas-y-Bryn Chalet Park

Bontnewydd
Nr Caernarfon
LL54 7YE
Tel: (01286) 672811

This small park is situated 2 miles from the historic town of Caernarfon. Set into a walled garden it offers safety, seclusion and beautiful views of Snowdonia. It is ideal for touring the area. Village pub and shop nearby. Choice of two or three bedrooms.

🐕	SP	WEEKLY RATES		No. OF CARAVANS	
				STATIC	HIRING
		MIN £	MAX £	14	10
		65.00	230.00	OPEN 3 - 12	

TC | Bryn Gloch Caravan & Camping Park

Betws Garmon,
Caernarfon, LL54 7YY
Tel: (01286) 650216
Fax: (01286) 650216

One of the most picturesque sites in Wales overlooked by the Snowdonia Mountain Range on bank of River Gwyrfai. Mount Snowdon only 2 miles. Ancient town of Caernarfon 5 miles, Isle of Anglesey and Llŷn Peninsula 30 minute drive. As a local family we insist that the site is kept clean and quiet and that people return time and time again. Voted Best Campsite Wales 1992. On site we have fishing, children's play area, games room, miniature golf, bar and restaurant. Within 15 minute drive pony trekking, beach boating and canoeing. 30 minutes dry ski slope and paragliding. SAE for brochure.

🐕 🍴		PER NIGHT		PITCHES	STATIC
⊡ ✕				TOURING 42	15
🍺 ⚬		MIN £	MAX £	M/VANS 50	OPEN
⌂ ⊙		6.00	8.00	TENTS 50	1 - 12

CP | Morfa Lodge Caravan Park

Dinas Dinlle,
Caernarfon
LL54 5TP
Tel: (01286) 830205
Fax: (01286) 831329

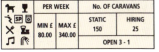

A friendly family run park located near a safe sandy beach and with superb views of Snowdonia mountains. Fully serviced luxury Dragon Award caravans, clubhouse with entertainment and family room. Heated outdoor swimming pool and children's play equipment, shop, launderette. Tourers and tents welcome. Caravans for sale. Telephone for free colour brochure.

🐕 🍴		PER WEEK		No. OF CARAVANS	
🏊 SP ⊡				STATIC	HIRING
✕ 🍺		MIN £	MAX £	150	25
🎵 ⌂		80.00	340.00	OPEN 3 - 1	

CP | White Tower Caravan Park

Llandwrog,
Caernarfon
LL54 5UH
Tel: (01286) 830649

Approx 3 miles from Caernarfon and 2 ½ miles from the beach. The park enjoys views of Snowdon and surrounding countryside. An ideal base for visiting Anglesey, Llŷn Peninsula or Snowdonia. Golf, horse riding, fishing, water sports all within 3 miles. Our new static six berth caravans offer luxury accommodation, alternatively we have a level touring field with all new modern shower/toilet facilities, including baby room and disabled room. All hot water is free.

🐕 🍴	WEEKLY RATES		No. OF CARAVANS	
🏊 ⊡			STATIC	HIRING
🍺	MIN £	MAX £	53	1
⌂	95.00	250.00	OPEN 3 - 10	

TC | Tyn yr Onnen Mountain Farm Caravan Park

Waunfawr,
Caernarfon, LL55 4AX
Tel: (01286) 650281
Fax: (01286) 650281

Long established 300 acre sheep farm with extensive mountain rights. Its seclusion, peaceful and tranquil surroundings offer solace and freedom, ideal for a relaxing or walking holiday. Ascent of Snowdonia peaks convenient from our site. Caernarfon, Isle of Anglesey and coast nearby. Games room and laundry. Modern shower/toilet block for tourers and campers. Shop, TV lounge/common room. Table tennis. Children's play area. Camp fires allowed. AA 2 pennants.

🐕 ⊡		PER NIGHT		PITCHES	STATIC
🍺 ⚬				TOURING 30	3
⌂		MIN £	MAX £	M/VANS 10	OPEN
		7.00	-	TENTS 40	1 - 12

Criccieth   Dolgellau   Dolwyddelan

SC   Betws-Bach Farm

Ynys,
Criccieth, LL52 OPB
Enquiries to: Mrs A. Jones
Tel: (01758) 720047
Tel: (01766) 810295
Fax: (01758) 720047

Truly romantic, memorable and special cottages to stay at and relax in comfort. Oak beams, inglenook log fires. microwave, dishwasher, washing machine. One cottage has a four-poster and sauna. Another boasts a Jacuzzi and another has its very own snooker table. All have large gardens with the freedom of 180 acres farmland with private fishing, rough shooting, wonderful walks, peace and quiet with Snowdonia and unspoilt beaches on our doorstep.

P	🐾	PER WEEK			SLEEPS
h	SP	MIN £	MAX £	FARMHOUSE	2 - 6 + COT
M	🛁	130.00	460.00	COTTAGE BUNGALOW	UNITS
		OPEN 1 - 12			3

SC   5 Star Cottage

Talhenbont Hall,
Talhenbont,
Criccieth
LL52 OLT
Enquiries to: Roger and Gillian Good
Tel: (01766) 810247

Lovingly restored stone cottage and hunting lodge in freedom of 70 acre wooded and rivered country estate. A luxurious and carefree holiday for the discerning. Available throughout the year. Woodland walks, wildlife and free tennis, riding and fishing. 1 mile from coast, 5 miles Snowdonia. Under the personal supervision of the owners.

P	🐾	PER WEEK			SLEEPS
h	SP	MIN £	MAX £	COTTAGES	2 - 10
M	🛁	175.00	975.00		UNITS
		OPEN 1 - 12			5

SC   Fridd

Roman Bridge,
Dolwyddelan
Enquiries to: Mr J. Palmer
Pont-y-Pant,
Dolwyddelan, LL25 OPQ
Tel: (01690) 750393 Ev, W/E
(01690) 750555 Day
Fax: (01690) 750544

Luxurious, beamed, secluded, old stone farmhouse with inglenook, log fire in peaceful Snowdonia valley. Beautiful views. Tourist paradise. 6 miles from Betws-y-Coed. Walking, many attractions, fishing, ½ hour from beaches, TV, video, microwave, washing machine, dryer.

P	h	PER WEEK			SLEEPS
SP	M	MIN £	MAX £	FARMHOUSE	2 - 9
🛁		150.00	350.00		UNITS
		OPEN 1 - 12			1

SC   Rocquebrune

c/o Glyn-y-Coed,
Porthmadog Rd,
Criccieth
LL52 OHP
Tel: (01766) 522870
Fax: (01766) 523341

Rocquebrune is a lovely family house surrounded by lawns and gardens with views of castles, sea and mountains. Sleeping 8 people, it has one ground floor bedroom and bathroom. Full gas heating and most modern equipment in the kitchen. Private parking, patio, verandah, make it an outstanding property.

P	🐾	PER WEEK			SLEEPS
h	SP	MIN £	MAX £	HOUSE/	8
M	🛁	100.00	575.00	BUNGALOW	UNITS
		OPEN 1 - 12			1

SC   Penmaenucha Farm

Penmaenpool,
Dolgellau
LL40 1YD
Tel: (01341) 423937

Properties situated overlooking the beautiful Mawddach estuary and mountains beyond. On a 600 acre sheep and beef farm extending up to the foothills of Cader Idris. Walking distance to George III hotel and RSPB lookout and reserve. Golden sandy beaches, pony trekking and fishing locally.

P	🐾	PER WEEK			SLEEPS
h	SP	MIN £	MAX £	FARMHOUSE	4 - 6
M	🛁	110.00	350.00	COTTAGE	UNITS
		OPEN 1 - 12			3

SC   Nant-yr-Haf

Roman Bridge,
Dolwyddelan
Enquiries to: Mrs M. Walters,
24 Prenton Hall Road,
Birkenhead,
Merseyside
L43 ORA
Tel: (0151) 6081065

AWAITING GRADING

A former school in the Lledr Valley, six miles from Betws-y-Coed. Lounge/dining room, two bedrooms, kitchen, bathroom. Excellent walking, country and many recreational facilities nearby.

h	SP	PER WEEK			SLEEPS
M	🛁	MIN £	MAX £	COTTAGE	4
		80.00	220.00		UNITS
		OPEN 1 - 12			1

Dolwyddelan   Dyffryn Ardudwy   Garndolbenmaen   Llanbedr   Llanbedrog

SC Ty'n-y-Ffos Bach

Dolwyddelan
LL25 0UJ
Tel: (01690) 750379
Fax: (01690) 750379

Delightful two bedroomed stone cottage in spectacular position overlooking Dolwyddelan and the beautiful Lledr Valley, opposite Moel Siabod with Snowdon Horseshoe beyond. On quiet, no through road, yet only 5 minutes walk from village. Beamed sitting room, original open fire, fully equipped. Pretty garden backing onto mountainside. Excellent walking. Special weekend arrangements November - Easter.

P	🐾	PER WEEK			SLEEPS
h	SP	MIN £	MAX £	COTTAGE	4/5
M		95.00	275.00		UNITS
		OPEN 1 - 12			1

Castles and Historic Places
Beautifully produced full-colour guide to more than 140 historic sites. Castles, abbeys, country houses, prehistoric and Roman remains. Detailed maps.
£7 inc. p&p
(see 'Guides and Maps' at the end of the book)

SC Ynys

Ystumgwern Hall Farm,
Dyffryn Ardudwy
LL44 2DD
Tel: (01341) 247249
Fax: (01341) 247171

Beautifully renovated 16th century cottages and barn conversions on 1,000 acre working farm. Sleeps 1-8 people in 1, 2, 3 and 4 bedroomed units. Within 6 miles pony trekking, bird watching, golf, walks, rivers, lakes, mountains, steam trains, castle and sandy beaches. De Luxe grade B&B also available from same units. Enquiries to John and Jane Williams.

P	🐾	PER WEEK			SLEEPS
h	SP	MIN £	MAX £	FARMHOUSES	1 - 8
📖		120.00	440.00	COTTAGES	UNITS
		OPEN 1 - 12			7

SC Riverside Holiday Bungalows

Llanbedr
LL45 2NW
Enquiries to: Mr & Mrs Wheatley
Tel: (01341) 241223
Fax: (01341) 241506

Small private site of 2/3 bedroom bungalows. Situated in picturesque Artro valley 300 yards from village. Central heating, fitted carpets/kitchens, colour TV, fridge, shower, microwave and conventional ovens. Sandy beaches, mountains, fishing, golf, riding within 3 miles or try the site's superbly equipped fitness centre. SAE please.

P	🐾	PER WEEK			SLEEPS
h	SP	MIN £	MAX £	BUNGALOW	1 - 6
M		115.00	250.00		UNITS
		OPEN 1 - 12			6

SC Bodwrog

Llanbedrog,
Pwllheli
LL53 7RE
Tel: (01758) 740341

Working farm. Superb coastal views, sandy beach 1 ½ miles. Colour television, radio, microwave, electric blankets, double glazing. Children welcome. Free babysitting, rough shooting. Watersports, riding, golf, sporting clays locally. Leisure centre 5 miles. Spring/Autumn breaks: Two nights £55.00, three £70.00, four £80.00. Bed linen, electricity included. Many returning guests. Croeso.

P	🐾	PER WEEK			SLEEPS
	SP	MIN £	MAX £	FARMHOUSE	5 - 6 COT PROVIDED
		110.00	260.00		UNITS
		OPEN 2 - 12			1

SC Rhinog Park

Beach Road,
Dyffryn Ardudwy
LL44 2HA
Tel: (01341) 247652
Fax: (01341) 247652

A warm welcome awaits on this quiet, select, family run retreat offering Scandinavian and cedarwood lodges furnished to a high standard. With superbly maintained grounds achieving five tick grading of excellence, the park is situated in an area of outstanding beauty between mountains and sea. Between the pretty harbour town of Barmouth and Harlech, it is ideally situated for golf, walking, sailing, riding, fishing and is just minutes stroll from golden beaches of Cardigan Bay.

P	🐾	PER WEEK			SLEEPS
SP	M	MIN £	MAX £	CHALETS	2 - 5 + COT
📖		95.00	295.00		UNITS
		OPEN 3 - 10			6

SC Melin Llecheiddior

Garndolbenmaen
LL51 9EZ
Tel: (01766) 530635
Fax: (01766) 530635

Situated near the River Dwyfach, within easy reach of sea and mountains. One double room, sun lounge, bathroom, lounge with colour TV, kitchen fully equipped, microwave. children welcome. Cot and high chair available. Pets welcome, on request. Leisure centre and riding stables nearby.

P	🐾	PER WEEK			SLEEPS
SP	M	MIN £	MAX £	COTTAGE	4
		95.00	125.00		UNITS
		OPEN 1 - 12			1

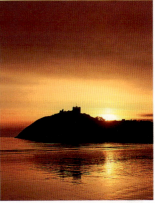

Criccieth Castle

Llanrwst Morfa Nefyn Nefyn

SC 6 Ty Plant

Nebo Road,
Llanrwst.
Enquiries to: E. Kerry Jenkins
Bodnant, Nebo Road,
Llanrwst, LL26 0SD
Tel: (01492) 640248/640683

Cosy stone cottage overlooking stream, ¼ mile from market town of Llanrwst and River Conwy. Ideal centre for exploring mountains and beaches of Snowdonia, with climbing, walking, pony trekking, golf and nature watching. Cottage consists of 2 bedrooms, dining room/lounge, stone fireplace and exposed beams, with hanging jugs. Kitchen, bathroom with shower. Off road parking, small garden. Cottage has been modernised but retains its old world charm. Local owner resides nearby. 7 berth house & B&B available. *i*

P	h	PER WEEK		SLEEPS
SP	M	MIN £	MAX £	5
	h	155.00	220.00	COTTAGE	UNITS
		OPEN 1 - 12		1

TC Glyn Farm Caravans

Trefriw,
Nr Llanrwst
LL27 0RZ
Tel: (01492) 640442

Small select family run site, centrally situated Snowdonia and coastal resort. Beautiful scenery, lovely walks, various outdoor activities nearby. Warm welcome awaits you. Situated Betws-y-Coed to Conwy B5106 road, turn into village car park opposite woollen mills, site 200 yds from main road. Static caravans available for hire from £160.00 per week.

		PER NIGHT	PITCHES	
		MIN £	MAX £	TOURING	STATIC
		6.50		28	6
			OPEN 3 - 10		

SC Garreg Lwyd

Morfa Nefyn,
Pwllheli, LL53 8UR
Enquiries to: Mrs M. Davies,
Caerwylan, Morfa Nefyn,
Pwllheli, LL53 6BW
Tel: (01758) 720572
or (01758) 720684

Well equipped accommodation on peaceful working farm. Five minutes by car from beautiful beaches, shop, golf, riding and fishing. 3 bedrooms, bathroom, lounge, colour TV, dining room, fully fitted kitchen, fridge-freezer, microwave, 3 oiled filled radiator, spin dryer, pantry, double glazed all through. Cleanliness and comfort assured. Children welcome. Large garden, plenty of parking space. Cot and high chair available.

P	h	PER WEEK		SLEEPS
h	SP	MIN £	MAX £	6
M		80.00		FARMHOUSE	UNITS
		OPEN 1 - 12		1

SC Beach Bungalow

The Beach,
Pontllyfni,
Caernarfon, LL54 5ET
Tel: (01286) 660400

A delightful beach bungalow moments from the beach. Area of outstanding natural beauty. Split level lounge, dining room, bathroom, 4 bedrooms, every comfort. Tastefully furnished. Teletext colour TV, video, CD music centre, dishwasher, microwave, fridge/freezer, washer, tumble dryer, phone, electric blankets, central heating 70°. Parking 5 cars, fishing, swimming, water sports, walking on flat coastal strip. Nearby restaurants, bar snacks, PO shop, 3 leisure centres. Tour beautiful Snowdonia, featured by BBC and WTB. View any time. Try a £49 minibreak now. Phone for brochure. *i*

P	h	PER WEEK		SLEEPS
h	SP	MIN £	MAX £	10
		89.00	499.00	BUNGALOW	UNITS
		OPEN 1 - 12		1

SC Trygarn

Bryn Glas,
Nefyn,
Pwllheli
LL53 6HT
Tel: (01758) 720596

Modern 3 bedroomed semi-detached house on outskirts of village, with open views. Fully equipped, clean and comfortable. Only 2 minutes from shops, maritime museum and children's playing area. Near sandy beach, golf course and hills. Large garden and parking space. Bed linen provided.

i

P	h	PER WEEK		SLEEPS
M		MIN £	MAX £	6
		120.00	265.00	HOUSE	UNITS
		OPEN 5 - 9		1

CP Beach Holiday West Point

Pontllyfni,
Caernarfon
LL54 5ET
Tel: (01286) 660400

Welcome to our world by the sea. Beach villa chalet, new super 12ft wide caravans. Your own beach moments from patio door, quiet seclusion, every comfort, luxury lounge overlooking lawn, beach and sea, lounge suite, dining room table and chairs, 1, 2 or three bedrooms, bathroom, teletext colour TV, microwave, electric blankets and bedroom heater. Free electric and gas. Well heated to 70°. Adjacent parking, boating, fishing, bathing, nearby restaurants, bar snacks. Featured by BBC and WTB, view anytime. Try a £12 mini break now. Brochure. *i*

	SP	PER WEEK		No. OF CARAVANS
		MIN £	MAX £	STATIC	HIRING
		49.00	199.00	50	50
			OPEN 3 - 10		

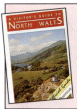

SC | Ael-y-Bryn

Morfa Bychan,
Porthmadog,
Enquiries to: Mr & Mrs Williams,
Penclogwywyn, Borth Road,
Porthmadog LL49 9UP
Tel: (01766) 512242

Four bedroomed residence overlooking golf course. Secluded setting with views of sea and hills 2 miles from Porthmadog. Amenities include golf, sailing, walking, steam railways. BLack rock beach 1 mile. Safe bathing. Sleeps six.

		PER WEEK			SLEEPS
P	🐕	MIN £	MAX £	HOUSE	6
h	SP	250.00	400.00		UNITS
		OPEN 1 - 12			1

CP | Greenacres Holiday Park

Black Rock Sands,
Morfa Bychan,
Porthmadog
LL49 9YB
Fax: (01766) 512084
Central Reservations: (0345) 125931

Greenacres is a Welsh Holidays Park, set in beautiful countryside and renown for its location as being one of the best in the British Isles. Wild mountain ranges and perfect beaches on your doorstep. Greenacres offers excellent family facilities, indoor heated pool, restaurant, bar and evening entertainment, pitch 'n' putt and multicourts. For a free full colour brochure call (0345) 125931 or contact your local travel agent. *i*

		WEEKLY RATES		No. OF CARAVANS	
				STATIC	HIRING
	SP	MIN £	MAX £	915	220
		99.00	469.00		
			OPEN 3 - 10		

SC | S.C. Gwynfryn Farm

Pwllheli
LL53 5UF
Tel: (01758) 612536
Fax: (01758) 614324

Visit an environmentally friendly area, where the Welsh language still flourishes. Come to our organic dairy farm, away from the "madding crowd", yet only 2 miles Lŷn's Heritage Coast. Castles, slate/copper mines, Snowdonia within 25 miles. Quality cottages for romantic couples or parties 4-8.Beds made up, cooked dishes to order, central storage heating, three with open fires, cleanliness and comfort assured. Launderette, telephone on site. Short breaks. Colour brochure. Early booking essential. *i*

		PER WEEK	HOUSES	SLEEPS
P	🐕	MIN £	MAX £	FARMHOUSES	2 - 8
h	SP	94.00		BUNGALOWS	UNITS
M		OPEN 1 - 12	MAISONETTES	8

SC | Felin Parc Cottages

Tanlan, Llanfrothen,
Penrhyndeudraeth, LL48 6HS
Enquiries to:
Mr & Mrs O.R. Williams-Ellis,
4 Sylvan Road, London SE19 2RX
Tel: (0181) 653 3118

Idyllic 17th century riverside Millhouse and charming detached cottage between Porthmadog and Beddgelert in beautiful private waterfall valley. Superior self-contained accommodation, fully modernised bathrooms, kitchens, colour TV. Secluded patios overlooking Mill Falls and Fording Bridge. Snowdon, Ffestiniog Railway, Portmerion all nearby. Winter mini breaks.

		PER WEEK			SLEEPS
P	🐕	MIN £	MAX £	MILLHOUSE	10 + 6
h	SP	150.00	550.00	COTTAGE	UNITS
M		OPEN 1 - 12			2

Porthmadog

Pwllheli   Tywyn

SC | Marinaland

Pwllheli
Enquiries to: Mrs M. Jones
Bryn Tani,
Llannor,
Pwllheli LL53
Tel: (01758) 701157

Comfortable accommodation in the beautiful Llŷn Peninsula. Ideal centre for touring and walking. Balcony off the lounge overlooks Snowdonia and the Pwllheli Marina. Also within a minute's walk from the beach. Pets welcome.

P h SP		PER WEEK		SLEEPS
		MIN £	MAX £	HOUSE	6
		120.00	340.00		UNITS
		OPEN 3 - 12			2

DRAGON AWARD

 The Dragon Award is your guide to the very best in individual caravan accommodation.

Award-winning caravans are extremely comfortable and luxuriously equipped – they include colour TV, heating and hot and cold water at no extra charge. Look out for the Dragon Award logo.

CP | Woodlands Holiday Park

Bryncrug,
Tywyn
LL36 9UH
Tel: (01654) 710471

Situated in the Snowdonia National park. Ideal for a family holiday. Two bedroom six berth caravans/chalets, equipped to high standards, on well established site. Each unit has shower/bath, fridge, colour TV. Site amenities include outdoor swimming pool, licensed country club, restaurant, laundry, mobile shop and touring site. Local attractions include fishing, walking, sailing and golf. Situated 3 miles from the coast on an elevated, hillside position.

		PER WEEK		SLEEPS	
				STATIC	HIRING
		MIN £	MAX £	122	16
		70.00	215.00		
				OPEN EASTER - 10	

SCA | Beresford Adams

The Harbour,
Abersoch,
Pwllheli
LL53 7AP
Tel: (01758) 712016
Fax: (01758) 713819

Abersoch and the Llŷn Peninsula. Personally inspected properties. Working closely with the Wales Tourist Board to ensure quality and comfort. Situated in Abersoch and the surrounding areas of this scenic peninsula to the southern tip of the North Wales coast. Numerous sandy beaches, rocky coves, golf courses, fishing. Snowdonia within one hour drive. Spring, autumn, winter short breaks available and why not try Christmas and New Year. Write or phone for brochure.

h SP M		PER WEEK		HOUSES FLATS COTTAGES BUNGALOWS CHALETS	SLEEPS
		MIN £	MAX £		2 - 10
		100.00	800.00		UNITS
		OPEN 3 - 12			60

Starcoast World, Pwllheli

This large area encompasses the rural heartlands of Wales. From the unexplored Berwyn Mountains in the north to the grassy heights of the Brecon Beacons in the south, the predominant colour is green. And the predominant mood is restful, for this is Wales's most peaceful and unhurried area, a place of quiet country roads and small market towns, hill sheep farms and rolling borderlands. It's also a place of scenic lakes — the Elan Valley, Clywedog and Vyrnwy – set in undisturbed landscapes rich in wildlife, where you may spot the rare red kite circling in the skies. And Wales's great outdoors doesn't come any greater than in the Brecon Beacons National Park, whose wide, open spaces were made for walking and pony trekking.

It's a fact…

The Brecon Beacons National Park, covering 519 square miles, was designated in 1957. The Beacons' peak of Pen-y-fan, at 886m/2907ft, is the highest summit in South Wales. The Elan Valley reservoirs, created between 1892 and 1903, were the first of Wales's man-made lakelands. Pistyll Rhaeadr, near Llanrhaeadr ym Mochnant, is the highest waterfall in England and Wales, plunging 73m/240ft. Sections of the 8th-century earthwork known as Offa's Dyke – the first official border between England and Wales – still stand almost to their full height in the hills around Knighton.

Mc1   Abergavenny

Flourishing market town with backdrop of mountains an south-eastern gateway to Brecon Beacons National Park. Pony trekking in nearby Black Mountains. Castle, Museum of Childhood and Home. Leisure centre. Monmouthshire and Brecon Canal runs just to the west. Excellent touring base for the lovely Vale of Usk and Brecon Beacons.

Ge6   Brecon

Main touring centre for the 519 square miles of the Brecon Beacons National Park. Handsome old town with thriving market, ruined castle, cathedral (with its imaginative Heritage Centre), priory, two interesting museums (Brecknock and South Wales Borderers') and Welsh Whisky Experience attraction. Wide range of inns and good shopping. Centre for walking and pony trekking. Golf, fishing, and canal cruising also available. Very popular summer International Jazz Festival.

Hb7   Crickhowell

Small, pleasant country town beautifully situated on the River Usk. Good for walking, fishing, pony trekking and riding. Remains of Norman castle, 14th-century Tretower Court and earlier castle worth a visit.

Hb5   Hay-on-Wye

Small market town on the Offa's Dyke Path, nestling beneath the Black Mountains on a picturesque stretch of the River Wye. A mecca for book lovers – there are antiquarian and second-hand bookshops, some huge, all over the town. Attractive crafts centre. Literature Festival in early summer attracts big names.

Eb5   Llanfair Caereinion

Pleasant town set amid rolling hills and forests in lovely Vale of Banwy. Best known as the terminus for narrow-gauge Welshpool and Llanfair Light Railway.

Eb3   Llanfyllin

Historic small country town in rolling peaceful farmlands at head of scenic Cain Valley. Undisturbed borderlands all around. Nearby Lake Vyrnwy and 73m/240ft Pistyll Rhaeadr waterfall are popular beauty spots. Also close to Welshpool and Powis Castle.

Ha6   Llangorse

Village in lovely pastoral location in Brecon Beacons National Park. Set at northern edge of Llangorse Lake with Mynydd Troed rising above. Popular with pony trekkers, walkers and sailors. A thriving activity holiday centre. Pleasant country inns and ancient church in village.

Gd1   Llanidloes

Historic and attractive market town at confluence of Severn and Clywedog rivers; excellent touring centre. Noted for its 16th-century market hall, now a museum, and other fine half-timbered buildings. Interesting shops. Massive Clywedog dam and lake 3 miles away on B4518. Take the scenic drive around lakeside and visit the Bryn Tail Lead Mine beneath the dam.

Dc5   Machynlleth

Historic market town near beautiful Dovey Estuary. Owain Glyndŵr's Parliament House in the wide handsome main street is now a museum and brass rubbing centre. Superbly equipped Bro Dyfi Leisure Centre offers wide range of activities. Celtica centre tells the story of Celtic myth and legend. Ancient and modern meet here; the inventive Centre for Alternative Technology is 3 miles away, just off the A487 to Dolgellau. Felin Crewi Flour Mill is off the A489 2 miles to the east.

Eb6   Newtown   ⇌

Busy Severn Valley market town and one-time home of Welsh flannel industry. Textile history recalled in small museum; another museum based around Robert Owen, pioneer socialist, who lived here. Town also has interesting W H Smith Museum, solid old buildings, river promenade, street market and the lively Theatr Hafren.

Ec5   Welshpool   ⇌

Old market town of the borderlands, full of character, with half-timbered buildings and welcoming inns. Attractive canalside museum. Good shopping centre; golf and angling. Powis Castle is an impressive stately home with a Clive of India Museum and outstanding gardens. Ride the narrow-gauge Welshpool and Llanfair Light Railway, visit the Moors Wildlife Collection.

Hc2   Presteigne

Typical black-and-white half-timbered border town with ancient inns; the Radnorshire Arms has secret passages. Pony trekking available – the perfect way to explore this tranquil wooded countryside. Offa's Dyke Path nearby.

Llangorse Lake

Hay-on-Wye (top)

Abergavenny   Brecon   Crickhowell   Hay-on-Wye

SC | Box Cottage

Mountainside,
Clydach,
Abergavenny,
Enquiries to: Mrs P.C. Pye,
High Trees,
Hancocks Mount,
Sunningdale,
Berks, SL5 9PQ
Tel: (01344) 20107

Box Cottage in the Brecon Beacons contains 2 bedrooms, sleeping 4. Log and coal stove. Situated at the edge of the village. Ideal for outdoor pursuits or total relaxation.

P h		PER WEEK			SLEEPS
		MIN £	MAX £	COTTAGE	4
		140.00	140.00		UNITS
		OPEN 4 - 10			1

SC | Tycerrig

Trallong,
Nr Brecon
LD3 8HP
Enquiries to: Mrs Bryer
Cae Parc, Trallong,
Nr Brecon LD3 8HP
Tel: (01874) 638848

Beamed stone cottage, renovated to a high standard with magnificent views of the Brecon Beacons. On the south facing slope of the Usk Valley.

P h		PER WEEK			SLEEPS
		MIN £	MAX £	COTTAGE	4
		110.00	200.00		UNITS
		OPEN 1 - 12			1

TC | The Orchard

The Bell Inn,
Glangrwyne,
Crickhowell,
NP8 1EH
Tel: (01873) 810247

AWAITING GRADING

Quiet, flat orchard at the rear of the Bell Inn, on A40 between Abergavenny and Crickhowell in Brecon Beacons National Park. Close to the Black Mountains, an area of outstanding natural beauty. Ideal walking country. Hang-gliding, sailing, pony trekking, fishing all nearby. Private stretch of trout fishing on River Usk.

		PER NIGHT		PITCHES	STATIC
		MIN £	MAX £	TOURING 5	-
		-	5.00	TENT PITCHES 5	OPEN 4 - 10

SC | Carno

Libanus,
Brecon
LD3 8NF
Tel: (01874) 625630
Fax: (01874) 625630

Highly recommended, beautifully restored, furnished and equipped 17th century farmhouse with original oak beams, inglenook fireplace and featured stone staircase. Has direct access into the Brecon Beacons National Park, one mile north west of Pen y Fan and five miles south of Brecon. Ideal for walking, bird watching. With golf, fishing, pony trekking, sailing close by. Castles, Mid Wales and coastal areas, all within easy reach.

P h SP M		PER WEEK			SLEEPS
		MIN £	MAX £	FARMHOUSE	4 / 5
		175.00	275.00		UNITS
		OPEN 1 - 12			1

SC | Pregge Mill

Pregge Lane,
Crickhowell,
NP8 1SE
Tel: (01873) 811157
Fax: (01873) 811157

Luxurious mill cottage overlooking Crickhowell. Ideal base for walking, golf, fishing, restaurants etc. Double glazed throughout. Double bedroom, shower room, sitting room on ground floor. Spiral stairway to forty foot lounge. Magnificent views. Modern kitchen with microwave, fitted carpets, garden, utility cum drying room. Short breaks available.

P h SP		PER WEEK			SLEEPS
		MIN £	MAX £	COTTAGE	2 - 5
		170.00	230.00		UNITS
		OPEN 1 - 12			1

SC | 6 The Village Cottage

Clyro,
Hay-on-Wye,
Enquiries to: G. Osborne,
27 Holly Rd,
Handsworth,
Birmingham, B20 2BU
Tel: (0121) 523 5323

Listed Jacobean cottage, in the rolling Wye Valley 1 ½ miles from Hay-on-Wye, Europe's biggest second hand bookshop. Share the peace of the old stone walls in the back garden, the fascination of the church where Kilvert wrote the best passage of his diary. For the adventurous, canoe on the Wye, sail at Llangorse, pony trek nearby or even parascend. All will enjoy delicious pub meals or unspoilt black and white villages.

P h M		PER WEEK			SLEEPS
		MIN £	MAX £	COTTAGE	5
		80.00	220.00		UNITS
		OPEN 1 - 12			1

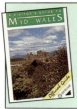

Llanfair Caereinion Llanfyllin Llangorse Llanidloes Llanrhaeadr ym Mochnant Machynlleth Merthyr Tydfil

---

SC Madog's Wells

Llanfair Caereinion,
Welshpool
SY20 0DE
Tel: (01938) 810446

Tastefully furnished bungalow, located on small hill farm in beautiful secluded valley. Two 6/8 berth, self-contained caravans available, £125 - £160 pw. Free gas/electricity, linen. Farmhouse, B&B, £14 per person. Picnic benches, games room, children's play area. Ideal for touring Mid Wales. Astronomy with superb 16" Dobsonian Telescope and NGC max computer.

P h SP 🐕	PER WEEK				SLEEPS
	MIN £	MAX £	BUNGALOW		5 + COT
	125.00	220.00			UNITS
OPEN 1 - 12					1

TC Lakeside Caravan and Camping Park

Llangorse Lake,
Brecon
LD3 7TR
Tel: (01874) 658226
Fax: (01874) 658430

Beautifully situated, friendly park with full facilities for touring caravans, motor homes and tents. It is an ideal base for exploring Mid and South Wales. Pony trekking nearby. Water sports, fishing and country fun. Well stocked shop, licenced club and cafe. Small outdoor swimming pool. Well equipped modern holiday caravans for hire.

	PER NIGHT		PITCHES	STATIC
	MIN £	MAX £	TOURING 10	75
				OPEN
	6.00	8.00	M/VANS 15	
			TENTS 15	4 - 10

SC Moelfre View

Darowen,
Machynlleth
SY20 8NU
Enquiries to: Mrs N. Wigley,
Rhosdyrnog, Talywern,
Machynlleth, SY20 8NU
Tel: (01650) 511288

Cottage of character situated in a quiet rural village amongst glorious unspoilt countryside. Seven miles from the market town of Machynlleth. Ideal base for walking, bird watching and exploring Mid Wales. Well equipped kitchen has microwave, cooker, fridge and spindryer. Garden furniture.

P h SP 🐕 M	PER WEEK			SLEEPS
	MIN £	MAX £	COTTAGE	4
	105.00	180.00		UNITS
OPEN 1 - 12				1

SC Clematis Cottage

Enquiries to: Mrs C. Spencer,
Rhoslan, Brithdir,
Llanfyllin SY22 5HB
Tel: (01691) 648339

Llanfyllin is surrounded by beautiful and peaceful unspoilt countryside; green hills and valleys, woodland and rivers. The cottage has much character and is conveniently situated in a narrow street, a few minutes walk from both shops and countryside. Lake Vyrnwy, Berwyn Mountains, Pystyll Rheadr Waterfall and Powys Castle all nearby.

h M	PER WEEK			SLEEPS
	MIN £	MAX £	COTTAGE	2 - 4
	75.00	175.00		UNITS
OPEN 1 - 12				1

SC Brelgwyn & Tŷ Bychan Cottages

The Rank, Cwmbelan,
Llanidloes
Enquiries to: J. Barratt,
18 Meadow Road,
Aldridge, Walsall,
West Midlands WS9 0ST
Tel: (01922) 52687

Tastefully restored cottages with open fires, beamed ceilings and lawned gardens, riverbank setting. Leisure facilities close by, superb for fishing, sailing, golf, walking. Renowned Red Kite country waiting to be discovered. Ideal family accommodation. SAE for brochure.

P h SP M	PER WEEK			SLEEPS
	MIN £	MAX £	COTTAGES	4 / 5
	100.00	170.00		UNITS
OPEN 3 - 11				2

SC Granary Cottages and Stable Flat

Ystradgynwyn,
Torpantau,
Merthyr Tydfil
CF48 2UT
Tel: (01685) 383358

Attractive stone farm buildings, offering comfortable self-catering accommodation in the Brecon Beacons National Park. 1000ft spectacular mountain scenery, reservoirs, rivers and waterfalls. Ideal for walking, cycling and bird watching, relaxed and peaceful atmosphere. Private parking. Safe for children. Short breaks when available. Merthyr Tydfil 6 miles, Brecon 15 miles.

P h SP M	PER WEEK		COTTAGES	SLEEPS
	MIN £	MAX £	FLAT	1 - 5
	125.00	250.00		UNITS
OPEN 1 - 12				3

SC Old Vicarage Cottage

Llangorse,
Brecon
LD3 7UB
Enquiries to: Mrs Anderson
Tel: (01874) 658639

Fully self-contained, semi-detached cottage in lovely quiet garden. A short walk from shops and pubs. Facilities include colour TV, full central heating, fully equipped kitchen. Children and well behaved dogs welcome. Within easy walk of lake. Sailing, fishing, pony trekking and walking can be enjoyed nearby.

P h SP M	PER WEEK			SLEEPS
	MIN £	MAX £	COTTAGE	4
	120.00	250.00		UNITS
OPEN 1 - 12				1

SC Glanllieriog

Caer Fach,
Llanrhaeadr ym Mochnant,
Oswestry
SY10 0DT
Tel: (01691) 791418

Comfortable detached bungalow ideally situated on a working farm on the Shropshire/Welsh border. Bed linen and all fuel included. Ample parking. Microwave, colour television, automatic washer/dryer, central heating. Garden with barbecue and picnic table. 4 bedrooms, 1 double, 1 twin, 2 single. One pet by arrangement.

P h SP 🐕	PER WEEK			SLEEPS
	MIN £	MAX £	BUNGALOW	6
	100.00	270.00		UNITS
OPEN 1 - 12				1

Newtown   Presteigne   Welshpool

SC | Port House Wood Cabins

Llanllwchaiarn
Nr Newtown
Enquiries to: Myrtle Villa,
Llanfair Road,
Newtown
SY16 2DL
Tel: (01686) 626856

Two luxury log cabins, furnished for comfort and convenience, ideal for superb holidays all year. Situated in a woodland with an abundance of wildlife and enjoying a quiet location, yet only 1 1/2 miles from Newtown. Ideal area for walking and private fishing on the River Severn. ℹ️

P 🐕		PER WEEK			SLEEPS
SP M		MIN £	MAX £	CHALETS	4
		105.00	150.00		UNITS
		OPEN 1 - 12			2

SC | Lords Building Farm

Leighton,
Nr Welshpool
Enquiries to: Mrs M.E. Edwards
Halfway House,
Nr Shrewsbury,
Shropshire, SY5 9EJ
Tel: (01743) 884356

Delightful stone farmhouse set in 73 acres of picturesque country. Modernised and well equipped. 3 bedrooms, kitchen, electric cooker and Aga, dining room, sitting room, bathroom with shower, storage heaters, pay phone, colour TV. Everything provided except linen. Car essential, 4 miles to Welshpool. Ideal touring base. Children and pets welcome. Leisure centre, cinema, canal.

P 🐕		PER WEEK			SLEEPS
h M		MIN £	MAX £	FARMHOUSE	7
		150.00	150.00		UNITS
		OPEN 3 - 10			1

SCA | Brecon Beacons Holiday Cottages

Brynoyre,
Talybont on Usk,
Brecon
LD3 7YS
Tel: (01874) 676446
Fax: (01874) 676416

Brecon Beacons, Black Mountains. Wide selection superbly situated traditional and unusual cottages and farmhouses sleeping from 2-30 with listed medieval tower, watermill, signal box. Comfortable cottages close to outdoor pursuits, walking, pony trekking, fishing, bird watching, mountain biking. Waterfalls, lakes, rivers, valleys, mountains. Excellent village pubs, good food, peaceful and quiet hideaways. Please telephone for brochure and to discuss individual properties.

🐕 h	PER WEEK		HOUSES	SLEEPS
SP	MIN £	MAX £	FARMHOUSES FLATS	2 - 30
	100.00	1250.00	COTTAGES	UNITS
	OPEN 1 - 12		BUNGALOWS	150

SC | Corner House

c/o Upper House,
Kinnerton,
Presteigne
LD8 2PE
Tel: (01547) 560207

Delightful cosily furnished black and white/stone cottages, particularly suited to off-season breaks, with fitted carpets and storage heaters. Its pine furnished kitchen includes electric cooker, microwave, fridge and automatic washing machine. The comfortable lounge has colour TV and open fire. The suntrap garden is secure for children and pets. Ample parking. Kinnerton, in the unspoilt Radnor Valley, 2 miles - Offa's Dyke, is an ideal base for touring Mid Wales and the beautiful borderland. ℹ️

P 🐕	PER WEEK			SLEEPS
h SP	MIN £	MAX £	COTTAGE	5 + 2
M	80.00	220.00		UNITS
	OPEN 1 - 12			1

Prices

For self-catering accommodation (furnished properties and caravan holiday home parks) rates are **PER UNIT PER WEEK.** For touring caravan and camping parks, rates are for **TWO PEOPLE** and their caravan, motorhome or tent **PER NIGHT.** All prices include VAT. Prices and other specific details were supplied to the Wales Tourist Board during June–September 1995. So do check all prices and facilities before confirming your booking.

Welshpool and Llanfair Light Railway

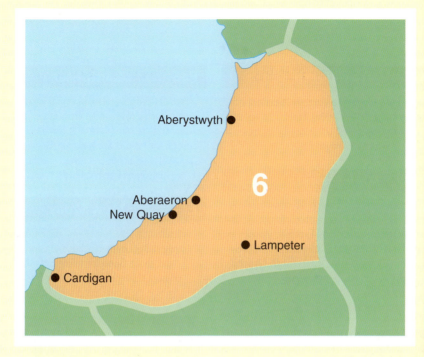

The southern arc of Cardigan Bay is dotted with pretty little ports and resorts, the

largest of which is Victorian Aberystwyth with its splendid seafront. Long sections of this seashore have been designated Heritage Coast, including the exposed headland of Ynys Lochtyn near Llangrannog where on stormy days it almost seems as if you are sailing away from the mainland on board a ship. Inland, you'll discover traditional farming country matched by traditional country towns. Venture a little further and you'll come to the Cambrian Mountains, a compelling wilderness area crossed only by the occasional mountain road. The Teifi Valley, in contrast, is a gentle, leafy landscape famous for its beautiful river scenery, falls and coracle fishing.

It's a fact…

Dylan Thomas took much of his inspiration for the fictitious seatown of Llareggub in *Under Milk Wood* from New Quay. Remote Strata Florida Abbey, Pontrhydfendigaid, was known as the 'Westminster Abbey of Wales' in medieval times. Aberystwyth's Cliff Railway, opened in 1896, is Britain's longest electric-powered cliff railway. The scenic Teifi Valley was once Wales's busiest woollen making area – a few mills still survive. The coracle, a tiny, one-man fishing boat used in Wales for 2000 years, can still be seen on the waters of the Teifi.

Ceredigion – Cardiganshire Coast and Countryside

Fa5   Aberporth

Popular seaside village. Two attractive beaches with swimming and good sea fishing. Scenic cliff walks. Convenient for visiting other coastal villages along Cardigan Bay.

Fe2   Aberystwyth   ≼

Premier resort on the Cardigan Bay coastline. Fine promenade, cliff railway, camera obscura, harbour and many other seaside attractions. Excellent museum in restored Edwardian theatre. University town, lively arts centre with theatre and concert hall. National Library of Wales stands commandingly on hillside. Good shopping. Vale of Rheidol narrow-gauge steam line runs to Devil's Bridge falls.

Fb4   Cwm Tudu

Picturesque away-from-it-all hamlet hidden away on coast near New Quay with lovely little beach beneath grassy headlands. Wonderful cliff walks.

Fe5   Lampeter

Farmers and students mingle in this distinctive small country town in the picturesque Teifi Valley. Concerts are often held in St David's University College, and visitors are welcome. Golf and angling, range of small shops and some old inns. Visit the landscaped Cae Hir Gardens, Cribyn.

Fc4   New Quay

Picturesque little resort with old harbour on Cardigan Bay. Lovely beaches and coves around and about. Good for sailing and fishing. Resort sheltered by protective headland.

The beach at Aberporth

Devil's Bridge falls (top)

Aberporth   Aberystwyth

SC Penffynnon Properties

Aberporth,
Cardigan
SA43 2DA
Tel: (01239) 810387
Fax: (01239) 811401

Our comfortable properties are next to Aberporth's two sandy beaches whose safe bathing waters are among the cleanest in Europe. We have ample parking. Dogs welcome by arrangement. The village has several pubs and a range of shops. Local attractions include Cardigan Bay Dolphins, water sports, golf, riding and walking in the Preseli Hills.

P 🏠		PER WEEK			SLEEPS 2 - 6
h SP		MIN £	MAX £	FLATS	
M ♿		100.00	300.00	BUNGALOWS	UNITS
		OPEN 1 - 12			7

CP Pilbach Caravan Park

Betws Ifan,
Rhydlewis,
Llandysul
SA44 5RT
Tel: (01239) 851434

A friendly welcome at our family owned park with our outdoor heated swimming pool, indoor games room, playing field and dog walk. High quality Dragon Award homes. Ideal for either a short break or a family holiday. Beautiful park like setting, 14 1/2 acres divided by trees and hedging into small paddock with close cut grass. Tourers and tents welcome, plenty of hook-ups. 3 1/2 miles from safe, sandy, clean beaches.

🐕 ♟		PER WEEK		No. OF CARAVANS	
⚲ SP		MIN £	MAX £	STATIC	HIRING
🔲 ✕		105.00	225.00	70	6
🏆		OPEN 3 - 10			

SC Aberleri Farm Cottages

Freepost Dept WSC
Aberleri Farm Cottages,
Cambrian Coast Park,
Borth
SY24 5JU
Tel: (01970) 871233
Fax: (01970) 871856

Re-built farmhouse and four cottages, all luxuriously appointed, in landscaped grounds with indoor swimming pool (plus Jacuzzi and children's play pool). Satellite TV, barbecue, children's outdoor play area. Sandy 'Blue Flag' beaches and golf course within 10 minute walk. Nature reserve adjacent. Borth village 1 mile. Use of facilities at nearby top-graded 'Dragon Award' holiday park. Shop, bar, catering, family entertainment, children's activities including fun pool with water-chute, go-karts, bouncy castle, indoor play areas, organised games. Ideal touring base.

P h		PER WEEK			SLEEPS 2 - 10
SP		MIN £	MAX £	FARMHOUSE	
		99.00	549.00	COTTAGES	UNITS
		OPEN 1 - 12			5

SC Geuallt Cottage

Old Goginan,
Nr Aberystwyth SY23 3PD
Enquiries to: G. Duffield
28 Newfield Rd,
Hagley, Nr Stourbridge,
West Midlands, DY9 0JU
Tel: (01562) 885097

Pretty white washed cottage located in tranquil setting 7 miles inland from Aberystwyth. Comfortable and cosy atmosphere having traditional stone walled living room with beams. Colour TV, car parking. Picnic area. An ideal base for those who enjoy walking, bird watching, fishing or just a holiday in a restful country environment.

P 🐕		PER WEEK			SLEEPS 4
M		MIN £	MAX £	COTTAGE	
		180.00	230.00		UNITS
		OPEN 5 - 10			1

CP Clarach Bay Holiday Village

Clarach Bay,
Nr Aberystwyth
SY23 3DT
Tel: (01970) 828277
Fax: (01970) 828003

Long established holiday village with every amenity for the perfect family seaside holiday. Luxury caravans with free gas, electricity, fitted kitchen, shower, flush toilets, colour TV. Private beach and trout stream, licenced club, cabaret, pool, amusements, shops, restaurants, putting green. Programme of entertainment. Resident greencoats. Sporting and sightseeing tours arranged.

🏆 ⚲		PER WEEK		No. OF CARAVANS	
🎵	✕	MIN £	MAX £	STATIC	HIRING
	♞	50.00	300.00	220	60
				OPEN 4 - 10	

SC Neuadd Farm Cottages

Llwyndafydd,
SA44 6BT
Enquiries to:
Malcolm and Karina Headley
Tel: (01545) 560324
Fax: (01545) 560324

Picture book stone cottages close to Cwm Tudu Cove and NT coast, seals and dolphins. Exceptional accommodation. Log fires, lovely gardens and grounds, heated swimming pool, peaceful meadows, lake. Pigmy goats, pony, donkey, ducks, Wendy House, play tractor. Village inn for good food just down the lane. Superb colour brochure.

P 🐕		PER WEEK			SLEEPS 2 - 6
h SP		MIN £	MAX £	COTTAGES	
🔲		200.00	700.00		UNITS
		OPEN 1 - 12			10

Cwm Tudu   Lampeter   New Quay

SC | Gaer Cottages

Cribyn,
Nr Lampeter
SA48 7LZ
Tel: (01570) 470275

Quality self-catering accommodation for all the family with an emphasis on facilities for disabled visitors. Nestling into beautiful unspoilt countryside, six of the nine traditional Welsh stone cottages are single storeyed, easily accessible from the large car park. Luxurious purpose built heated indoor swimming pool and games room. Open all year. Groups welcome.

		PER WEEK		SLEEPS 3 - 9
P	🐕	MIN £	MAX £	
h	SP	150.00	550.00	COTTAGES
		OPEN 1 - 12		UNITS 9

Pets welcome

You'll see from the symbols that many places to stay welcome dogs and pets by prior arrangement. Although some sections of beach may have restrictions, there are always adjacent areas – the promenade, for example, or quieter stretches of sands – where dogs can be exercised on and sometimes off leads. Please ask at a Tourist Information Centre for advice.

CP | Quay West Holiday Park

New Quay.
SA45 9SE
Tel: (0345) 422422
Fax: (01545) 560016
Central Reservations: 01545 560608

Quay West is a Welsh Holidays Park, situated around the friendly village of New Quay, overlooking the harbour, and enjoying panoramic views across Cardigan Bay with its beautiful beaches and mountain backed shore. British Holidays always ensures excellent family entertainment and facilities; heated pool, restaurant, bar and evening entertainment. For a free brochure call (0345) 422422 or contact your local travel agent.

	PER WEEK		No. OF CARAVANS	
	MIN £	MAX £	STATIC	HIRING
SP	99.00	434.00	629	223
	OPEN 3 - 1			

Cwm Tudu, near New Quay

Fishguard
St David's
7
Haverfordwest
Pembroke
Saundersfoot
Tenby

Pembrokeshire is traditionally known as *gwlad hud a lledrith*, 'the land of magic and enchantment'. Anyone who has visited the sandy bays around Tenby, for example, or the breathtaking sea-cliffs at Stack Rocks, or the rugged coastline around St David's will agree with this description. Pembrokeshire is one of Europe's finest stretches of coastal natural beauty. Not surprisingly, it's also a haven for wildlife. Wildflowers grow on its cliffs, seals swim in its clear waters, and seabirds nest in huge numbers all along the coast. Pembrokeshire's stunning coastal beauty extends inland to the Preseli Hills, an open expanse of highland scattered with mysterious prehistoric sites. And away from the coast you'll also discover castles and a host of places to visit.

It's a fact…

The Pembrokeshire Coast National Park covers 225 square miles and runs from Poppit Sands near Cardigan in the north to Amroth in the south. It was created in 1952. The park's symbol is the razorbill, a reflection of the prolific seabird populations to be found here. The Pembrokeshire Coast Path, opened in 1970, runs for 186 miles. The park's boundary clings to the coast except in one instance, when it dips inland to encompass the Preseli Hills, which rise to 536m/1760ft. The Dale Peninsula is the sunniest place in Wales.

Fa6 Aber Cych

Hamlet near Cenarth beside the Afon Cych where it flows into the Teifi. Beautiful riverbanks, excellent fishing. Woollen mills, romantic ruined castle, wildlife centre and Cardigan Bay resorts nearby.

Jb5 Broad Haven

Sand and green hills cradle this holiday village on St Bride's Bay in the Pembrokeshire Coast National Park. Beautiful beach and coastal walks. National Park Information Centre.

Fa5 Cardigan

Market town on mouth of River Teifi close to beaches and resorts. Good shopping facilities, accommodation, inns. Golf and fishing. Base for exploring inland along wooded Teifi Valley and west to the Pembrokeshire Coast National Park. Y Felin Corn Mill and ruined abbey at neighbouring St Dogmael's. Welsh Wildlife Centre nearby.

Je4 Clunderwen

Centrally located for all of Pembrokeshire. The national park's northern, western and southern shores are all within easy reach of this village, which stands in countryside just south of the Preseli Hills. Llawhaden Castle, Black Pool Mill Caverns and Oakwood Park all close by.

Jb3 Croes-goch

Small village, useful spot for touring Pembrokeshire Coast National Park – especially its peaceful, rugged northern shores and nearby centres of St David's and Fishguard. Llangloffan Farmhouse Cheese Centre nearby.

Jc2 Fishguard

Lower Fishguard is a cluster of old wharfs and cottages around a beautiful harbour. *Under Milk Wood* with Richard Burton was filmed here in 1971. Shopping in Fishguard town. Good walks along Pembrokeshire Coast Path and in the country. Nearby Goodwick is the Irish ferry terminal, with a direct link from London. Excellent range of craft workshops in area including Tregwynt Woollen Mill. Music Festival in July.

Jc5 Haverfordwest

Ancient town – now a good base for exploring the Pembrokeshire Coast National Park – and the administrative and shopping centre for the area. Medieval churches and narrow streets. Museum in the castle grounds, which occupy an outcrop overlooking the town. Attractive redeveloped riverside and old wharf buildings. Picton Castle a few miles to the east. Many other attractions nearby, including Scolton Manor Country Park, 'Motormania' exhibition, Selvedge Farm Museum and Nant-y-Coy Mill.

Lower Fishguard harbour

Jb5 Little Haven

Combines with Broad Haven – just over the headland – to form a complete family seaside holiday centre in the Pembrokeshire Coast National Park. The village dips down to a pretty sandy beach. Popular spot for sailing, swimming and surfing.

Jd4 Llys-y-fran

Village in the centre of Pembrokeshire, near the old county town of Haverfordwest. Llys-y-fran Reservoir and Country Park provides amenities for watersports, fishing and walking. There is more superb walking in the nearby Preseli Hills.

Jd6 Manorbier ⇌

Described as 'the most pleasant spot in Wales' by that much-travelled priest Gerald of Wales 800 years ago, this unspoilt village on the coast of south Pembrokeshire near Tenby has an imposing Norman castle. Sandy bay and fine coastal walks are among its attractions.

Je5 Narberth ⇌

Small market town, ancient castle remains (private). Charming local museum. Convenient for beaches of Carmarthen Bay and resorts of Tenby and Saundersfoot. Many attractions nearby, including activity-packed Oakwood Park, Canaston Centre, Heron's Brook Country Park, Folly Farm and Blackpool Mill.

Jd6 Pembroke ⇌

Ancient borough built around Pembroke Castle, birthplace of Henry VII. In addition to impressive castle, well-preserved sections of old town walls. Fascinating Museum of the Home. Sandy bays within easy reach, yachting, fishing – all the coastal activities associated with estuaries. Plenty of things to see and do in the area, including visit to beautiful Upton Castle Grounds.

Ja4 St David's

Smallest cathedral city in Britain, shrine of Wales's patron saint. Magnificent ruins of a Bishop's Palace beside ancient cathedral nestling in hollow. Set in Pembrokeshire Coast National Park, with fine beaches nearby; superb scenery on nearby headland. Craft shops, sea life centres, painting courses, boat trips to Ramsey Island, farm parks and museums; ideal for walking and birdwatching.

Je1 St Dogmael's

Near Cardigan on the Teifi Estuary with good fishing and coastal walking. Site of ancient abbey and working flour mill, beaches nearby. Ideal for touring north Pembrokeshire and the Cardigan Bay coast.

Je6 Saundersfoot ⇌

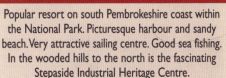

Popular resort on south Pembrokeshire coast within the National Park. Picturesque harbour and sandy beach. Very attractive sailing centre. Good sea fishing. In the wooded hills to the north is the fascinating Stepaside Industrial Heritage Centre.

Jb4 Solva

Pretty Pembrokeshire coast village with small perfectly sheltered harbour and excellent craft shops. Pembrokeshire Coast Path offers good walking. Famous cathedral at nearby St David's.

Je6 Tenby ⇌

Popular, picturesque south Pembrokeshire resort with two wide beaches. Fishing trips from the attractive Georgian harbour and boat trips to nearby Caldy Island. The medieval walled town has a maze of charming narrow streets and fine old buildings, including Tudor Merchant's House (National Trust). Galleries and craft shops, excellent museum on headland, good range of amenities. Attractions include Manor House Wildlife and Leisure Park and 'Silent World' Aquarium.

Abercych   Broad Haven   Cardigan   Clunderwen   Croes-goch   Fishguard

SC The Mews

Clynfyw,
Abercych,
Boncath,
Pembrokeshire,
SA37 0HF
Tel: (01792) 473736 or (01239) 841236

Spacious, well equipped, mews cottage in large grounds. Sleeps 6. A bedroom and bathroom on level ground floor, ideal for the infirm. Table tennis room. Convenient for Cardigan Bay Beaches, Preseli Hills, riding and fishing schools. Peaceful surroundings, woodland walking and abundant bird life. Solid fuels and bed linen included. **i**

P		PER WEEK			SLEEPS
h	M	MIN £	MAX £		6
		175.00	235.00	COTTAGE	UNITS
		OPEN 1 - 12			1

SC Millmoor Farm Cottages & Rocksdrift Aparts

Broad Haven,
Haverfordwest,
Pembrokeshire
SA62 3JH
Tel: (01437) 781507
Fax: (01437) 781002

Prince of Wales Award Winning accommodation in heart of Pembrokeshire Coast National Park. Superb beach and Heritage Coastline 200 yards. Well kept gardens and play area. Personally run and supervised by owners who care! WTB Gold Medal Winners. Disabled welcome. Please write or phone anytime for free colour brochure. **i**

P		PER WEEK			SLEEPS
h	SP	MIN £	MAX £	FLATS	2 - 8
		99.00	645.00	COTTAGES	UNITS
		OPEN 1 - 12			24

DISCOVERING ACCESSIBLE WALES
The above publication is packed full of helpful information for visitors with disabilities. Subjects covered include attractions, accommodation and activities. For your free copy please see 'Guides and Maps' at the end of the book.

SC Llantood Farm Cottages

Llantood,
Cardigan
SA43 3NU
Tel: (01239) 612537

Situated on 200 acre working farm 3 miles south of Cardigan and 3 miles from the coast. These 18th century cottages are ideal for exploring the Pembrokeshire Coast National Park. The 3 cottages have been carefully renovated to the highest standards and provide luxury accommodation including microwave, fridge/freezer, washing machine, inglenook and exposed beams. Each cottage has its own secluded fenced garden with patio black. Visitors welcome to explore farm and 30 acres of woodland. Brochure Mrs G. Evans. **i**

P		PER WEEK			SLEEPS
h	SP	MIN £	MAX £		2 - 6
M		120.00	330.00	COTTAGES	UNITS
		OPEN 1 - 12			3

SC Gwarmacwydd Farm

Llanfallteg
SA34 0XH
Tel: (01437) 563260
Fax: (01437) 563839

A working farm of 400 acres, Gwarmacwydd is idyllically situated in the wooded Vale of the River Taf. Within 20 minutes of the sandy beaches of Tenby and Saundersfoot, Gwarmacwydd's character stone cottages are a comfortable, centrally heated and well equipped base from which to explore West Wales.

P		PER WEEK			SLEEPS
h	SP	MIN £	MAX £		2 - 6
		100.00	395.00	COTTAGES	UNITS
		OPEN 1 - 12			5

SC Y Lodge

Trearched Farm,
Croes-goch,
Haverfordwest
SA62 5JP
Tel: (01348) 831310

18th century, listed, single storey lodge cottage at farm drive entrance on A487, village outskirts. Small garden. Footpath link through farm to Trefin approx 2 1/4 miles. Ideal touring, walking, bird watching. Sorry no dogs. Village shop/Post office, 200 yards. B&B available in farm guesthouse. Short breaks October to Whitsun.

P		PER WEEK			SLEEPS
SP		MIN £	MAX £		2
		80.00	160.00	COTTAGE	UNITS
		OPEN 1 - 12			1

SC Brynawel Country House

Llanwnda,
Goodwick,
Pembrokeshire
SA64 0HR
Tel: (01348) 874155

Cottage adjoins Victorian guest house farm, sheep, poultry, coastal path, golf, pony trekking, various fishing nearby. Strumble Head "Hide" rare migratory birds, beach and coves accessible. Lawned patio, barbecue, linen. Duty free ferry to S. Ireland. B&B available in farm house. Free brochure on request. Owners personal attention. Great welcome.

P		PER WEEK			SLEEPS
h	SP	MIN £	MAX £		4
M		100.00	260.00	COTTAGE	UNITS
		OPEN 1 - 12			1

Prices

In this publication we go to great lengths to make sure that you have a clear, accurate idea of prices and facilities. It's all spelled out in the 'Prices' section – and remember to confirm everything when making your booking.

SC | 2 Park View

Rope Walk, Fishguard
Pembrokeshire, SA65 9BT
Enquiries to: Beryl Badland
Llain-yr-Esgob,
Dwrbach, Fishguard,
Pembrokeshire, SA65 9RR
Tel: (01348) 873685

A cosy well furnished cottage close to the centre of Fishguard, offering holiday freedom to those who appreciate the comforts of independence and access to the spectacular Pembrokeshire coastline. Ideally situated overlooking an attractive park with children's play facilities and free parking at rear. One double bedroom, one twin bedroom. Brochure on request.

		PER WEEK			SLEEPS 4
		MIN £	MAX £	COTTAGE	
		90.00	210.00		UNITS
		OPEN 1 - 12			1

SC | Cleddau Lodge

Camrose,
Haverfordwest,
SA62 6HY
Tel: (01437) 710226

Large Georgian part house sleeping 7 with hot and cold in all bedrooms, living room, colour TV, kitchen and bathroom. Separate entrance. Car spaces. Farm cottage sleeping 4-5 with colour TV. Children welcome. All set on 50 acre estate with gardens, woodlands and river fishing. 6 miles coast. B&B also available.

		PER WEEK			SLEEPS 4 - 7
		MIN £	MAX £	HOUSE	
		100.00	250.00	COTTAGE	UNITS
		OPEN 3 - 10			2

SC | Lower Cottage

Slatemill, Dale Road,
Haverfordwest,
Enquiries to: Mrs Crabtree,
164 London Rd,
Aston Clinton, Aylesbury,
Bucks HP22 5LB
Tel: (01296) 630602

Comfortable, fully modernised, beamed farm cottage, privately situated within the Pembrokeshire Coast National Park. Close to Marloes, Dale, Little Haven and other beautiful beaches and havens.

		PER WEEK			SLEEPS 6
		MIN £	MAX £	COTTAGE	
		160.00	220.00		UNITS
		OPEN 4 - 10			1

CP | Fishguard Bay Caravan Park

Dinas Cross,
Newport
SA42 0YD
Tel: (01348) 811415

Enjoy superb views along this unspoiled coastline. Our quiet, family run park, situated within the Pembrokeshire Coast National Park, is an ideal base for walking and touring this beautiful corner of Wales. Several beaches, horse riding, tennis, golf and many other attractions nearby.

		PER WEEK	No. OF CARAVANS	
			STATIC	HIRING
		MIN £	MAX £	50	12
		110.00	300.00		
		OPEN 3 - 12			

SC | Haven Cottages

Whitegates,
Little Haven,
Haverfordwest,
SA62 3LA
Tel: (01437) 781552
Fax: (01437) 781552

Situated 200 metres from lovely sandy beach with safe bathing and interesting rock pools, close to shops and local eating places. Ideal for bird watching, golf, fishing, wind surfing or family beach holiday. Small sheltered gardens, pets welcome, linen provided.

		PER WEEK			SLEEPS 2 - 12
		MIN £	MAX £	COTTAGES	
		95.00	490.00		UNITS
		OPEN 1 - 12			5

SC | Stoneleigh Cottage

Ambleston,
Haverfordwest,
Pembrokeshire
SA62 5RD
Tel: (01437) 731423

Delightful stone cottage (not isolated), very comfortable and well equipped, cot, high chair, linen provided, colour TV, central heating, log fire (optional). Large garden, with barbecue/picnic area. The cottage is very central for exploring the entire Pembrokeshire coastline with beautiful sandy beaches. Two country parks with walks and picnic areas nearby, and delightful Preseli Hills. Also riding, fishing and golf. Many families return annually. A warm welcome assured. Brochure on request.

		PER WEEK			SLEEPS 5 + COT
		MIN £	MAX £	COTTAGE	
		95.00	250.00		UNITS
		OPEN 1 - 12			1

Haverfordwest   Little Haven   Llys-y-fran   Manorbier

SC   No 3 Woodlands

Cuffern, Nr Roch,
Haverfordwest,
Pembrokeshire,
Enquiries to: M. J. Hill,
15 Netherstone Grove,
Sutton Coalfield, B74 4DT
Tel: (0121) 3539430

Comfortably furnished modern chalet, delightful woodland site between St David's and Haverfordwest. Many safe, sandy beaches. Fishing, boating, golf, walking, riding all within easy reach by car. All electric. Sleeps 4, one double room, one twin bedroom. Sitting/dining room, TV, electric heaters, kitchen,cooker, fridge, immersion heater. Fully fitted bathroom. Car park space.

P h			SLEEPS
M			4
	MIN £	MAX £	CHALET
	85.00	165.00	
	OPEN 4 - 10		UNITS
			1

CP   Scamford Caravan Park

Keeston,
Haverfordwest,
Pembrokeshire
SA62 6HN
Tel: (01437) 710304

Our peaceful park is situated in attractive countryside near Newgale beach, the Pembrokeshire Coastal Path and the island bird sanctuaries. Only 25 luxury caravans, with all mains services, showers and colour TV. Excellent children's playground. Dog welcome (some caravans "dog free"). 5 touring pitches, with electric hook-ups, hot showers.A warm welcome from the resident owners.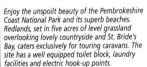

		PER WEEK	No. OF CARAVANS
			STATIC	HIRING
		MIN £	MAX £	25	25
		90.00	310.00	
		OPEN 4 - 10		

SC   Little Haven Cottages

Woodlands Farm
and Walton West Farm,
Little Haven,
Haverfordwest
Pembrokeshire
Enquiries to: Mrs Judith Stephens,
St George's, Tidenham, Chepstow NP6 7JF
Tel: (01291) 623337
Fax: (01291) 627631

Walk down to the superb sandy beaches from two groups of holiday cottages perched above the fishing village of Little Haven. Converted stone built and slated barns and farmhouses with private gardens. Some have a beautiful sea view and all have car parking, colour TV, heating, tumble dryer and modern fitted kitchen. Cots and highchairs. Pets welcome by arrangement.

P	h		PER WEEK			SLEEPS
h	SP					2 - 12
M			MIN £	MAX £	COTTAGES	
			75.00	650.00	FARMHOUSE	UNITS
			OPEN 1 - 12			13

TC   Redlands Touring Caravan Park

Little Haven,
Haverfordwest,
Pembrokeshire
SA62 3UU
Tel: (01437) 781301

Enjoy the unspoilt beauty of the Pembrokeshire Coast National Park and its superb beaches. Redlands, set in five acres of level grassland overlooking lovely countryside and St. Bride's Bay, caters exclusively for touring caravans. The site has a well equipped toilet block, laundry facilities and electric hook-up points.

		PER NIGHT		PITCHES	STATIC
					-
		MIN £	MAX £	TOURING	
		6.00	7.00	M/VANS } 60	OPEN
					4 - 9

SC   Ivy Court Cottages

Ivy Court,
Llys-y-fran,
Nr Haverfordwest,
Pembrokeshire, SA63 4RS
Tel: (01437) 532473
Fax: (01437) 532473

A private hamlet of delightful traditional cottages (featured on TV's "Wish You Were Here") nestling on the hillside above the lake of Llys-y-fran Country Park which offers super scenery, fishing and walking. You can easily tour the entire National Park Coast from this central rural location or simply relax in our award winning grounds. An all-weather pavilion spans our heated swimming pool. Restaurant nearby. Pubs, riding 3 1/2 miles. Children welcome. Brochure on request.

P	h		PER WEEK			SLEEPS
h	SP					2 - 7
			MIN £	MAX £	COTTAGES	
			100.00	490.00		UNITS
			OPEN 1 - 12			10

SC   Aquarium Cottage & The Lobster Pot

Manorbier, Tenby,
Pembrokeshire SA70 7ST
Enquiries to: Mrs J. Hughes,
Rose Cottage, Manorbier,
Tenby, Pembrokeshire
Tel: (01834) 871408

Detached country cottage (sleeps 6) and pleasant ground floor flat (sleeps 4). Ample parking. Pets welcome, linen and electricity included in price. Both properties 1/2 mile village and sea. Brochure available.

P			PER WEEK			SLEEPS
						4 - 6
			MIN £	MAX £	FLAT	
			135.00	300.00	COTTAGE	UNITS
			OPEN 3 - 10			2

Manorbier   Narbeth   Pembroke   St David's

SC | Castle Cottages

Manorbier, Tenby,
Pembrokeshire, SA70 7SX
Enquiries to: Monica Calver
Gleann-na-Coille Pembroke Road,
Manorbier, Tenby, Pembrokeshire
Tel: (01834) 871559
Fax: (01834) 871559

Comfortably furnished, centrally heated cottages and bungalows set in mature secluded gardens in coastal village. ¼ mile from safe, sandy beach and famous Pembrokeshire Coast Path with spectacular views. Village inn, shop, bakery and restaurant nearby. Play area in village. Colour television, microwave, laundry, private parking. Ideal base for activities, walking, sailing, golf, horse riding.

P h M	SP	PER WEEK			SLEEPS 4 - 5 - 7
		MIN £	MAX £	COTTAGES	
		120.00	360.00	BUNGALOW	UNITS
		OPEN 1 - 12			4

SC | Green Grove

Jameston,
Manorbier,
Tenby,
Pembrokeshire
SA70 8QJ
Tel: (01834) 871245

Eight tastefully converted stone cottages and flats in spacious lawned surroundings with acres of room for children to play. Indoor heated pool, table tennis room. Launderette. Situated within the Pembrokeshire Coast National Park and ¾ mile from safe sandy beaches. The small village provides a shop, inn and petrol station and is within easy travelling distance of Tenby and Pembroke. Outdoor activities available in the area include walking, sailing, riding, golf etc.

P h	SP	PER WEEK			SLEEPS 2 - 6
		MIN £	MAX £	FLATS	
		100.00	380.00	COTTAGES	UNITS
		OPEN 3 - 10			8

SC | Landway Farm

Manorbier,
Nr Tenby,
Pembrokeshire
Enquiries to: Mrs S Thomas
Park Farm, Manorbier, Nr Tenby,
Pembrokeshire, SA70 7SU
Tel: (01834) 871264

Traditional farmhouse, sleeping 6 - 8. Large sunlounge, colour television, freezer, microwave, automatic washing machine, telephone, central heating. Walled garden, pets allowed. Suitable for disabled. Near coastal path for walking. Easy distance for shops, castles, beaches and many other activities.

P h		PER WEEK			SLEEPS 6 - 8
	M	MIN £	MAX £	FARMHOUSE	
		130.00	350.00		UNITS
		OPEN 5 - 9			1

SC | Grove Cottages

The Grove,
Molleston,
Narbeth
Pembrokeshire
SA67 8BX
Tel: (01834) 861190

Three self-catering cottages, barn and stable conversions, set in delightful countryside in Landsker Borderlands. Beach 20 minute drive. Centrally located within Pembrokeshire, yet very peaceful and secluded. Sleeps 2 - 5. Bed linen provided. Pets welcome free of charge.

P h M	SP	PER WEEK			SLEEPS 2, 4, 5
		MIN £	MAX £	COTTAGES	
		120.00	300.00		UNITS
		OPEN 1 - 12			3

TC | Windmill Hill Caravan Park

Windmill Hill Farm,
St Daniel's Hill
Pembroke
SA71 5BT
Tel: (01646) 682392

Situated one mile south of Pembroke town, this peaceful select caravan park is close to the famous Pembrokeshire National Park and coastline. The amenities provided on site include thirty level caravan pitches, ten motor caravan spaces and thirty tent pitches, some with electric points and a modern toilet and shower block.

		PER NIGHT		PITCHES	STATIC 70
		MIN £	MAX £	TOURING 30	
		4.00	10.00	M/VANS 10	OPEN 3 - 10
				TENT 30	

SC | The Bickney

Enquiries to: R.C. Moore
Idyllic Cottages of Pembrokeshire,
Penparc, Tre-fin,
Nr St David's
Pembrokeshire, SA62 5AG
Tel: (01348) 837865
Fax: (01348) 837865

One of our top quality selection of immaculate, clean and warm cottages set in beautiful coast and country locations. Our cottages are selected for their quiet and peaceful surroundings within or very close to the Pembrokeshire Coast National Park with its magnificent coastline and sandy beaches. For peace and quiet it has to be Pembrokeshire. Free colour brochure.

P h M	SP	PER WEEK		HOUSES FARMHOUSES	SLEEPS 2 - 10
		MIN £	MAX £	FLATS	
		99.00	660.00	COTTAGES	UNITS
		OPEN 1 - 12		BUNGALOWS	60

St David's   Saundersfoot   Solva

SC | Derwen Cottage

1 Lower Moor,
St David's
Pembrokeshire SA62 6RP
Enquiries to: L.M. Marlow,
140 Church Road,
Reading RG6 1HR
Tel: (01734) 266094

Charming stone cottage with panoramic views over the coast and offshore islands. Exceptional accommodation, washing machine, electric shower, colour television, luxury bedding, enclosed lawned garden, five bedrooms.

P h M	🐕 SP 🗄	PER WEEK		COTTAGE	SLEEPS 10
		MIN £ 90.00	MAX £ 500.00		UNITS 1
		OPEN 1 - 12			

TC | Lleithyr Farm Caravan Park

Nr Whitesand Bay,
St David's
Pembrokeshire
SA62 6PR
Tel: (01437) 720245

The caravan park is situated on the St David's peninsula 1 1/2 miles from the picturesque cathedral city and 1/4 mile from Whitesand Bay, making local amenities such as numerous cliff walks, surfing, golf, horse riding etc very accessible.

🐕 🐾	PER NIGHT		PITCHES	STATIC 40
	MIN £ 4.00	MAX £ 8.00	TOURING 20	
			M/VANS 5	OPEN 3 - 11
			TENTS 5	

CP | Saundersfoot Bay Leisure Park

Broadfield,
Saundersfoot,
Pembrokeshire
SA69 9DG
Tel:(01834) 812284
Fax: (01834) 813387

Situated on the beautiful Pembrokeshire Coast National Park coastline between Saundersfoot and Tenby, about ten minutes stroll from the beach, this award winning park commands magnificent views over Camarthen Bay. Our luxury holiday homes are fully equipped and every unit has full mains services, central heating, satellite TV, microwave oven, and fridge/freezer. Best Caravan Park in Britain - Calor Gas Award 1994. Prince of Wales Landscaping Award. Write or phone for colour brochure.

🐕 SP 🗄	PER WEEK		NO. OF CARAVANS	
	MIN £ 85.00	MAX £ 395.00	STATIC 165	HIRING 55
			OPEN 3 - 12	

SC | No Name Cottage

St David's
Pembrokeshire
Enquiries to: Quality Cottages,
Cerbid, Solva,
Haverfordwest,
Pembrokeshire, SA62 6YE
Tel: (01348) 837871

WTB Tourism Award Winners. One of a selection of quality cottages with exceptionally high residential standards. Log fires. Pets welcome free. All around the magnificent Welsh coastline with its numerous sandy beaches and superb scenic walks. A naturalist's paradise. Free colour brochure.

P h 🗄	🐕 SP	PER WEEK		HOUSES FARMHOUSES	SLEEPS 2 - 14
		MIN £ 280.00	MAX £ 790.00	FLATS COTTAGES	UNITS 150
		OPEN 1 - 12		BUNGALOWS	

SC | Waters Edge

The Strand,
Saundersfoot,
Pembrokeshire
SA69 9EX
Enquiries to: Mrs Joan Griffiths
Tel: (01834) 812617

Luxury holiday properties with magnificent coastal views and direct access to fine sandy beach providing safe bathing and excellent boating and fishing. All flats have private sun balconies, colour television, electric storage heating and parking space. Ideally situated for sailing, fishing horse riding, golf and generally exploring Pembrokeshire.

P h 🗄	🐕 SP	PER WEEK		FLATS	SLEEPS 3 - 7
		MIN £ 98.00	MAX £ 452.00		UNITS 12
		OPEN 3 - 12			

SC | Kingheriot Farm

Solva,
Haverfordwest,
Pembrokeshire
SA62 6XN
Tel: (01437) 721313

Working family farm situated in the outstanding beauty of the Pembrokeshire Coast National Park. 5 minutes from the hamlet of Solva, 10 minutes from the cathedral city of St David's. All home comforts available including colour television, video recorder, washing machine, microwave oven etc. Watersports, walking, pony trekking, beautiful beaches, fun parks all nearby.

P h M 🗄	PER WEEK		FARMHOUSE	SLEEPS 6 + COT
	MIN £ TOA	MAX £ TOA		UNITS 1
	OPEN 4 - 9			

SC | Llanddinog Farm Cottages

Solva,
Haverfordwest,
Pembrokeshire
SA62 6NA
Tel: (01348) 831224

Delightful luxury cottages grouped around farm courtyard, only 3 miles from sandy beaches, coastal paths. Fully equipped, centrally heated. Fishing, riding, watersports, golf, island trips, bird watching, seals and puffins. Colour TV, barbecue, large flowery garden, swings, small animals. Meals available. Cot, highchair provided. Short breaks. Pets welcome. Brochure. Mrs S. Griffiths.

P 🐕		PER WEEK			SLEEPS 4 - 6
h SP		MIN £	MAX £	COTTAGES	
M		120.00	425.00		UNITS 3
		OPEN 1 - 12			

SC | Carnock House Flatlets

c/o Clarence House Hotel,
Esplanade, Tenby,
Pembrokeshire
SA70 7DU
Tel: (01834) 844371
Fax: (01834) 844372

Quality sea front flatlets for two adults, self-contained within one family room. All electric, equipped dinette, colour TV, shower, toilet. Cliff garden steps opposite to South Beach. Top floor family flat sleeps four, close to walled town centre, shops, entertainment. Easy walking to car parking, coaches, trains. Clarence House amenities open to Carnock residents. Send now for free colour brochure/tariff.

🐕 h		PER WEEK			SLEEPS 2, 3, 4
SP	M	MIN £	MAX £	FLATS	
		55.00	245.00		UNITS 10
		OPEN 4 - 9			

CP | Cross Park Holiday Centre

Broadmoor,
Kilgetty,
Tenby,
Pembrokeshire, SA68 0RS
Tel: (01834) 811244/813205
Fax: (01834) 814300

Cross Park is one of Wales' leading family supervised holiday parks in eleven acres of parkland. A quality park for families and couples with a high percentage of repeat bookings and recommendations. Super facilities include family clubhouse with free nightly live entertainment, swimming pool, shop, restaurant/take away, games room, play area, launderette.

🐕 🍴		PER WEEK		No. OF CARAVANS	
SP		MIN £	MAX £	STATIC	HIRING
⏹ ✕		79.00	399.00	85	50
🎵				OPEN 3 - 10	

SC | Penally Riverside Cottages

Penally House,
LLandudoch,
Aberteifi
SA43 3HR
Tel: (01239) 615380

In the historic village of St Dogmael's, The Boat House, Alun Owen's Cottage and The Saddler's are on the banks of the River Teifi. A birdwatcher's paradise. Sailing, canoeing, fishing, walking, the Pembrokeshire Coast Path, Cardigan 1 mile. One bedroom cottages, two on one level.

P h		PER WEEK			SLEEPS 2
SP M		MIN £	MAX £	COTTAGES	
		155.00	363.00		UNITS 3
		OPEN 1 - 12			

SC | The Old Vicarage

Penally,
Tenby,
SA70 7PN
Tel: (01834) 842773

Comfortably furnished cottages and apartments in beautiful location overlooking Carmarthen Bay and Tenby Golf Course. Easy walk to large sandy beach. Central heating, colour television, microwave, laundry, telephone, large secluded garden, private parking. Walk along Pembrokeshire's famous coastal foot path with spectacular views. Colour brochure available.

P 🐕		PER WEEK		FLATS	SLEEPS 2 - 5
h SP		MIN £	MAX £	COTTAGES	
M		90.00	330.00		UNITS 7
		OPEN 1 - 12			

CP | Kiln Park Holiday Centre

Kiln Park,
Marsh Road, Tenby,
Pembrokeshire, SA70 7RB
Tel: (0345) 433433
Fax: (01834) 842437
Central Reservations: (01834) 844121

Kiln Park is a Welsh Holidays Park, set amongst the beauty of the Pembrokeshire Coast National Park, surrounded by stunning countryside and sandy beaches. The delightful resort of Tenby with its three excellent beaches, picturesque harbour and medieval town wall are only a stone's throw away. There is loads to do for all the family from Indoor Aqua Complex, fishing off the beach, amusements and bowling lanes, restaurant, bar and evening entertainment. For a free Welsh Holidays brochure call (0345) 433433 or contact your local travel agent.

🍴 🦢		PER WEEK		No. OF CARAVANS	
🐕 SP		MIN £	MAX £	STATIC	HIRING
✕ 🐾		119.00	550.00	719	186
🎵				OPEN 3 - 1	

Tenby

CP Lydstep Beach Holiday Park

Lydstep Haven,
Tenby,
Tel: (0345) 432432
Fax: (01834) 871871
Central Reservations: (01834) 871871

Lydstep Beach is a Welsh Holidays Park, set in a secluded bay and award winning beach bordered by the Pembrokeshire Coast National Park headland and sheltering woodland. British Holidays always ensures excellent family entertainment and facilities; heated outdoor pool, restaurant, bar and evening entertainment. For a free brochure call (0345) 432432 or contact your local travel agent.

	PER WEEK		No. OF CARAVANS	
			STATIC	HIRING
	MIN £	MAX £	466	117
	99.00	514.00		
			OPEN 3 - 11	

TC Masterland Farm Touring Caravan & Tent Park

Broadmoor,
Kilgetty,
Pembrokeshire, SA68 0RH
Tel: (01834) 813298
Fax: (01834) 814408

Small, friendly park, 2 miles Saundersfoot, 4 miles Tenby. First class facilities, hard standing for tourers on level grass pitches, separate area for tents and dormobiles. Both with electric hook-ups, children and pets welcome, baby bathroom, washing-up and food preparation facilities, play area, games room, TV room, library, launderette, barbecue. 6 berth caravan available, booking essential for high season. Brochure available from H. & M. Davies, resident proprietors. Touring caravan storage also available.

		PER NIGHT		PITCHES	STATIC
					1
		MIN £	MAX £	TOURING 13	OPEN
		3.75	11.00	M/VANS 10	3 - 10
				TENT 10	

SCA Coastal Cottages of Pembrokeshire

The Holiday
Information Centre
No 2 Riverside Quay,
Haverfordwest,
Pembrokeshire SA61 2LJ
Tel: (01437) 765765
Fax: (01437) 769900

Luxury cottages in the loveliest locations within the Pembrokeshire Coast National Park. There is a wide choice with something for everyone. Secluded stone cottages in sandy coves surrounded by National Trust land and modern properties close to family attractions, restaurants and pubs. Our free guide book and experienced staff make booking easy.

		PER WEEK		HOUSES	SLEEPS
				FARMHOUSES	2 - 12
		MIN £	MAX £	FLATS	
		130.00	850.00	COTTAGES	UNITS
		OPEN 1 - 12		BUNGALOWS	400

TC Cross Park Holiday Centre

Broadmoor,
Kilgetty,
Tenby,
Pembrokeshire
Tel: (01834) 813205/811244
Fax: (01834) 814300

Cross Park is a delightful family holiday park in eleven acres of landscaped gardens and lawns surrounded by mature trees and colourful shrubs and flowers. The award winning park has super facilities including family clubhouse with free nightly live entertainment, swimming pool, shop, restaurant/take away, launderette. Quality at an inclusive price.

		PER NIGHT		PITCHES	STATIC
					85
		MIN £	MAX £	TOURING 35	OPEN
		6.00	13.50	M/VANS 4	3 - 10
				TENT 12	

TC Trefalun Park

Devonshire Drive,
St Florence, Tenby
SA70 8RH
Tel: (01646) 651514
Freephone 0500 655314
Fax: (01646) 651746

Select family run park with first class facilities set in Pembrokeshire's beautiful countryside, minutes drive from the glorious beaches of Tenby and Saundersfoot. Grassy level paddocks for tourers and tents with electric hook-ups and super pitches. AA 3 pennants. Fully serviced Dragon Award caravans from £100 pw, low season. Heated outdoor swimming pool, licensed club, shop and coarse fishing lake available at adjoining park for small charge. Phone for free colour brochure.

		PER NIGHT		PITCHES	STATIC
					10
		MIN £	MAX £	TOURING 30	OPEN
		4.00	10.00	M/VANS 5	4 - 10
				TENT 25	

SCA Quality Cottages

Cerbid,
Solva,
Haverfordwest,
Pembrokeshire
SA62 6YE
Tel: (01348) 837871

WTB Tourism Award winners, 33 years experience in self-catering. We offer a selection of quality cottages with exceptionally high residential standards. Log fires etc, pets welcome free. Around the magnificent Welsh coastline with its numerous sandy beaches and superb scenic walks - a naturalist's paradise. Free colour brochure.

		PER WEEK		HOUSES	SLEEPS
				FARMHOUSES	2 - 14
		MIN £	MAX £	FLATS	
		110.00	840.00	COTTAGES	UNITS
		OPEN 1 - 12		BUNGALOWS	150

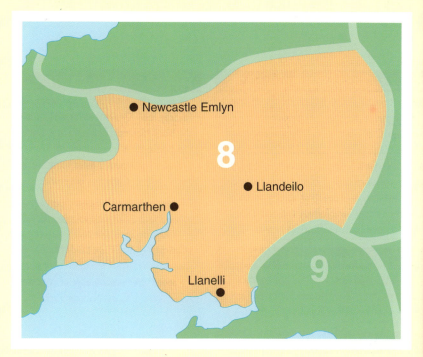

Dylan Thomas captured the essence of this timeless part of Wales in his short stories and poems, but most of all in his masterwork, *Under Milk Wood*. Dylan lived at Laugharne, a sleepy seatown set amongst the sweeping sands of Carmarthen Bay. Here you can wander along endless beaches, and then turn your attention to the patchwork of green farmlands which roll gently down to the sea. There's a rare sense of peace and tranquillity in the countryside around Carmarthen. Explore the lovely Vale of Towy, the moors of Mynydd Llanybydder or the glades of the Brechfa Forest. And don't miss market day at Carmarthen, or the view from the ramparts of Carreg Cennen, one of Wales's most spectacular castles.

It's a fact…

In the 1920s, the huge 6-mile beach at Pendine was used for land speed record attempts. Dolaucothi, Pumsaint, is the only place in Britain where we know, for certain, that the Romans mined for gold. The beach at Cefn Sidan, Pembrey, is 7 miles long. Twm Shôn Cati, Wales's answer to Robin Hood, hid in the hills north of Llandovery from the Sheriff of Carmarthen. Christmas mail can be postmarked from Bethlehem, a hamlet between Llandeilo and Llangadog.

Kc2 Carmarthen

Prosperous country town in pastoral Vale of Towy. Lively market and shops, livestock market. Carmarthen Castle was an important residence of the native Welsh princes but only the gateway and towers remain. Golf, fishing, tennis and well-equipped leisure centre. Remains of Roman amphitheatre. Immaculate museum in beautiful historic house on outskirts of town. Gwili Railway and ornamental Middleton Hall Amenity Area nearby.

Kc3 Ferryside

Village attractively set in off-the-beaten-track location on mouth of Towy Estuary, with views across the water to Llansteffan. Popular sailing centre.

Ga7 Llandeilo

Farming centre at an important crossing on River Towy, and handy as touring base for Carreg Cennen Castle, impressively set on high crag, and remains of Dryslwyn Castle. Limited access to Dinefwr Castle in magnificent parklands on edge of town. Gelli Aur Country Park nearby has 36 hectares/90 acres, including a nature trail, arboretum and deer herd.

Gb6 Llandovery

An important market town on the A40 with a ruined castle; its Welsh name Llanymddyfri means 'the church among the waters'. In the hills to the north is the cave of Twm Siôn Cati – the Welsh Robin Hood. Good touring centre for Brecon Beacons and remote Llyn Brianne area.

Ke1 Llanfynydd

Village deep in the country lanes between Llandeilo and Brechfa in green and peaceful setting. Fishing, walking and pony trekking countryside. Lakeside Talley Abbey, Brechfa Forest and beautiful Vale of Towy close by.

Ga6 Llangadog

Small market town set on two tributaries of the nearby Towy. Convenient for walking and touring the Black Mountain. The road over Black Mountain to Brynaman is one of the most scenic in South Wales. Bethlehem, 2 miles south, has a famous Christmas postmark.

Ka3 Pendine

Village on extensive beach and dunelands of Carmarthen Bay. Huge sandy beach – one of the largest in Wales – the site of record-breaking car speed attempts. On edge of Pembrokeshire Coast National Park.

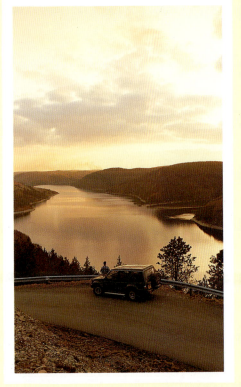

Llyn Brianne

SC | Byre Cottage

Troedyrhiw Country Guest
House and Holiday Cottage,
Llanfynydd,
Carmarthen
SA32 7TQ
Tel: (01558) 668792

*Set in glorious countryside, this cosy cottage is
part of a traditional Welsh farmhouse. 8 acres of
grounds with Jacob sheep and small vineyard.
The cottage has a double and single bedroom
with extra bed in lounge, with all you need for a
relaxing holiday. There are castles and coasts
nearby ready to be explored.*

	PER WEEK		SLEEPS 2 - 4
P SP h	MIN £ 90.00	MAX £ 220.00	COTTAGE
			UNITS 1
	OPEN 1 - 12		

SC | Cwmdwyfran Farm Cottage

Cwmdwyfran,
Bronwydd Arms,
Carmarthen
SA33 6JF
Tel: (01267) 281419

*A superb holiday cottage converted from a stone
farm building, comfortably equipped to a high
standard. South facing verandah, beautiful views.
An idyllic quiet setting. Abundant birdlife, ample
parking space. Fishing and Gwili Railway within
one mile. Golf, pony trekking and beaches within
a short drive. Assorted farm animals. Central for
touring.*

	PER WEEK		SLEEPS 4/5
P h	MIN £ 89.00	MAX £ 200.00	COTTAGE
M			UNITS 1
	OPEN 3 - 11		

SC | Cwm Farm Holiday Cottage

AWAITING GRADING

Cwm Farm,
Ferryside
SA17 5UF
Tel: (01267) 267519

*Farm holiday cottage and caravan at Carmarthen
Bay. See all the farm animals, feed the pet lambs,
milk the cows. Lyn the pig and Sam the sheepdog
are waiting to meet you. This holiday is a child's
paradise. Half a mile from sea and near the well
known Blue Flag beach in Pembrey Country Park.*

	PER WEEK		SLEEPS 8
P SP	MIN £ 141.00	MAX £ 176.25	COTTAGE
			UNITS 1
	OPEN 1 - 12		

Llansteffan Castle

SC | Maerdy Cottages

Taliaris, Nr Llandeilo,
Carmarthenshire, SA19 7DA
Enquiries to: Mrs Jones
Dan-y-Cefn, Manordeilo,
Nr Llandeilo, Carmarthenshire
Tel: (01550) 777448
Fax: (01550) 777067

*Situated near the Brecon Beacons these special
cottages enjoy privacy and quiet seclusion in
breathtaking unspoilt countryside. Each cottage
offers quiet comfortable interiors with
traditional furnishings, beams and log fires.
Perfectly located to discover the magnificent
beauty of Wales. Pony trekking, walking, bird
sanctuary nearby. Catering available. Brochure.*

	PER WEEK		SLEEPS 3,5,5,7,8,8
P h M	SP	MIN £ 200.00	MAX £ 600.00 COTTAGES
			UNITS 6
	OPEN 3 - 12		

Wales Tourist Map

- Our best-selling map now with a new look
- Detailed 5 miles/inch scale
- Wealth of tourist information
- 14 specially devised car tours
- Town plans
  £2 inc. p&p

(see 'Guides and Maps' at the end of the book)

TC | Erwlon Caravan and Campsite Park

Erwlon,
Brecon Road,
Llandovery
SA20 0RD
Tel: (01550) 720332

*A family run park beautifully located alongside a
babbling brook at the foothills of the Brecon
Beacons. The site provides the ideal base for a
touring holiday taking in the great natural
beauty which makes Wales so popular.
Conveniently located within 1 kilometre of
Llandovery. Ideal for the backpacker and
caravanner alike.*

	PER NIGHT		PITCHES	STATIC -
	MIN £ 6.00	MAX £ 6.00	TOURING 20 M/VANS 5 TENTS 15	OPEN 1 - 12

Llanfynydd   Llangadog   Pendine

SC Sannan Court

Llanfynydd,
Carmarthen, SA32 7TQ
Enquiries to: Hamdden Ltd,
Plas y Ffynnon, Cambrian Way,
Brecon LD3 7HP
Tel: (01874) 614657
Fax: (01558) 668190

Situated in the tranquil village off Llanfynydd, Sannan Court comprises of a Victorian House converted into five high standard, self-contained apartments of various sizes and Sannan Lodge converted from the adjacent barn which has two twin bedrooms, a magnificent lounge and private facilities. Nearby is a village shop and hostelry with further restaurants in the scenic Tywi Valley. Access to our salmon and sea trout fishing on the Afon Tywi available.

P h SP	PER WEEK		SLEEPS 2 - 6
	MIN £	MAX £	HOUSE
	120.00	550.00	FLATS
	OPEN 1 - 12		UNITS 6

CP Cross Inn & Black Mountain Caravan & Camping Park

Llanddeusant,
Llangadog
SA19 9YG
Tel: (01550) 740621

Small family site surrounded by the magnificent scenery of the Brecon Beacons National Park and glorious views towards the 2630 ft Fan Brycheiniog. This area of outstanding natural beauty offers the visitor numerous attractions. Excellent walking country, fishing and pony trekking close by. Ideally situated for touring South and Mid Wales. Quiet site.

SP	WEEKLY RATES		No. OF CARAVANS	
	MIN £	MAX £	STATIC	HIRING
	100.00	200.00	15	9
	OPEN 1 - 12			

CP Pendine Sands Holiday Park

Nr Carmarthen
SA33 4NZ
Tel: (0345) 443443
Fax: (01994) 453654
Central Reservations: (01994) 453398

Pendine is a Welsh Holidays Park, situated in the heart of Pendine village. Our park is adjacent to Pendine beach, famous for its world land speed record attempts. Explore the rock pools and coves and be captivated by the coastal scenery. British Holidays always ensures excellent family entertainment and facilities. Heated indoor swimming pool, family putting green, snack bar and evening entertainment. For a free brochure call (0345) 443443 or contact your local travel agent.

	PER WEEK		PER WEEK	
	MIN £	MAX £	STATIC	HIRING
	109.00	414.00	519	95
	OPEN 3 - 10			

Talley Abbey

The city of Swansea enjoys a wonderful location. It stands on the grand curve of Swansea Bay at the doorstep to the beautiful Gower Peninsula and green Vale of Neath. It's a maritime city through and through – there's even a stylish Maritime Quarter complete with marina and attractive waterside developments. Modern and traditional Wales mix happily in this friendly city. At its heart is a fresh foods market where you can buy welshcakes, laverbread and cockles from Penclawdd on Gower. The pretty little sailing centre of Mumbles stands at the gateway to Gower, a lovely peninsula with a string of sandy, south-facing bays and a towering curtain of cliffs. Inland, there are the waterfalls and forests of the Vale of Neath to explore.

It's a fact...

In 1956, the Gower Peninsula was the first part of Britain to be declared an 'Area of Outstanding Natural Beauty'. Swansea Museum, Wales's oldest museum, dates from the 1830s. The inaugural meeting of the Welsh Rugby Union was held at Neath in 1881. The waterwheel at the National Trust's Aberdulais Falls is Europe's largest electricity-generating waterwheel. The traditional Welsh delicacy known as laverbread (a kind of puréed seaweed) is usually eaten as an accompaniment to bacon and eggs.

Kd5   Horton

Seaside Gower village near Port-Eynon with an extensive sandy beach. Some of Gower's most spectacular cliff scenery close by.

Kc5   Rhosili

Gower's spectacular 'Land's End', a village set on headland above stunning 3 miles of sandy beach. Good surfing, hang gliding, coastal walking. A strange formation known as Worms Head juts into sea. National Trust Visitor Centre.

Kc5   Llangennith

Wales's surfing centre. Huge west-facing beach along Rhosili Bay very popular with surfers – whatever the weather! Road from village leads down through the dunes to this vast beach, on tip of Gower Peninsula. Whiteford Burrows to the north, clifftop Rhosili and spectacular promontory of Worms Head to the south.

Worm's Head

Port-Eynon (top)

Rhosili beach

SC Westernside Farm Bungalows

Horton, Gower,
Swansea
Enquiries to: John Baxter,
Pennard Hill Cottage,
Parkmill, Swansea, SA3 2EH
Tel: (01792) 371301

Situated on a quiet park overlooking Port Eynon Bay on the beautiful Gower Peninsula, our two bedroom bungalows are superbly furnished and equipped. Cots and highchairs available. Clean, safe, sandy beach ½ mile. Superb area for walking, riding, golf, watersports, sea fishing and bird watching. Please write or phone for full details including short breaks.

P h SP 🖥	🐕	PER WEEK		BUNGALOWS	SLEEPS 4
		MIN £	MAX £		
		150.00	270.00		UNITS 6
OPEN 3 - 12					

SC Annie's Stables

AWAITING GRADING

Middleton,
Rhosili, Gower
Enquiries to: Mrs B. Howe
Old Farmhouse,
Middleton, Rhosili,
Gower, SA3 1PJ
Tel: (01792) 390560

Converted, furnished traditional barn with uninterrupted views over cliffs. It is 750m to clean, safe bathing beach. The cottage is well equipped, centrally heated with south facing patio/garden. Ideally situated for walking, surfing, fishing, pony trekking, bird watching. Under personal supervision of owners who live nearby.

P h	🐕 M	PER WEEK		COTTAGE	SLEEPS 5 + COT
		MIN £	MAX £		
		180.00	320.00		UNITS 1
OPEN 4 - 10					

SC West End Cottage

The Cross, Llangennith,
Gower, Swansea
Enquiries to: Mrs M.H. Waters
16 Penlan Crescent,
Glanmor,
Swansea, SA2 0RL
Tel: (01792) 298448

Comfortable family holiday cottage in Gower village. One mile from beautiful sandy beaches and magnificent coastal scenery. Large garden with lovely view. Ideal centre for walking, birdwatching and fishing.

P h SP	🐕	PER WEEK		COTTAGE	SLEEPS 6
		MIN £	MAX £		
		180.00	200.00		UNITS 1
OPEN 5 - 10					

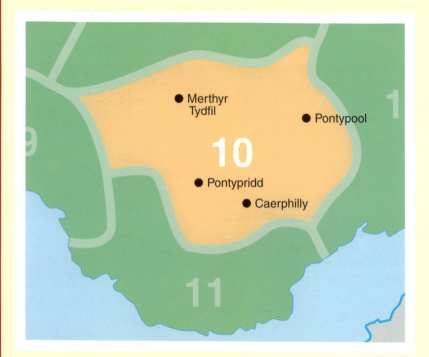

The Valleys of South Wales

The Valleys of South Wales are full of surprises – dramatic natural beauty, country and wildlife parks, forest and cycle trails, and a huge range of attractions. Did you know that Caerphilly Castle is regarded as one of Europe's greatest surviving examples of medieval military architecture? Or that there's a scenic narrow-gauge railway which takes you into the foothills of the Brecon Beacons from Merthyr Tydfil? Or that you can enjoy everything from walking to watersports at an exceptional range of country parks? Yet the past hasn't been entirely forgotten. Although the Valleys are green again, there's a rich industrial heritage at places like the Big Pit Mining Museum, Blaenafon, and the Rhondda Heritage Park, Trehafod.

It's a fact...

Caerphilly Castle, which covers 12 hectares/30 acres, is one of Britain's largest. Its 'leaning tower' out-leans Pisa's. In the 19th century, Merthyr Tydfil was Wales's largest town and the 'iron capital of the world'. The world's first steam engine, built by Cornishman Richard Trevithick, ran from Merthyr to Abercynon in 1804. There are around 15 country parks in the Valleys. Pontypridd is singer Tom Jones's home town. Blaenafon's Big Pit Mining Museum was a working colliery until 1980. The last coalmine in the Rhondda closed at the end of 1990.

Mb3   Blackwood

Southern valley town surrounded by pine-clad hills rising to mountain tops. Visit Penyfan Pond, a country park a few miles to the north, attractive Parc Cwm Darran and the Sirhowy Valley Country Park. Tour Llancaiach Fawr historic house and Stuart Crystal's glass factory nearby.

Ma2   Tredegar

Former ironmaking town in hilly 'Heads of the Valleys' close to the Brecon Beacons National Park – town's clocktower is made of iron. Attractive Bryn Bach Park and Parc Cwm Darran both nearby.

Le2   Merthyr Tydfil   ⇌

Once the 'iron capital of the world'. The museum in Cyfarthfa Castle, built by the Crawshay family of ironmasters and set in pleasant parkland, tells of those times. Visit the birthplace of hymn-writer Joseph Parry and the Ynysfach Engine House. The narrow-gauge Brecon Mountain Railway makes the most of the town's location on the doorstep of the Brecon Beacons National Park. Garwnant Forest Visitor Centre and scenic lakes in hills to the north.

Brecon Mountain Railway, Merthyr Tydfil   *Living history at Llancaiach Fawr manor house, near Nelson (top)*

Blackwood   Merthyr Tydfil   Tredegar

SC	Gelligoediog Holiday Cottages

Gelligoediog Farm,
Manmoel,
Blackwood
NP2 0RH
Tel: (01495) 246844 (day)
    (01495) 371097 (eve)
Fax: (01495) 249102

Situated near the sleepy hamlet of Manmoel on a working farm. These homely cottages are tastefully decorated and offer superb peaceful accommodation. Log burning stoves, fuel provided. Bed linen provided. Ideal base for exploring South Wales and its attractions. Well worth a visit.

P 🐕	PER WEEK			SLEEPS
h SP	MIN £	MAX £	COTTAGES	6
	175.00	200.00		UNITS
	OPEN 1 - 12			2

TC	Parc Bryn Bach

The Visitor Centre,
Merthyr Road,
Tredegar
NP2 3AY
Tel: (01495) 711816

Easily accessible panoramic site overlooking lake, set in 600 acres of country park. Ideally situated on the edge of the Brecon Beacons National Park and at the top of the historic South Wales Valleys. Signposted from the A465 Heads of The Valleys Road.

🐕 📷	PER NIGHT		PITCHES	STATIC
✕ 🍴			TOURING 15	-
⚠ 🔥	MIN £	MAX £	M/VAN 10	OPEN
	3.50	6.00	TENT PITCHES 5	1 - 12

Cyfarthfa Castle, Merthyr Tydfil

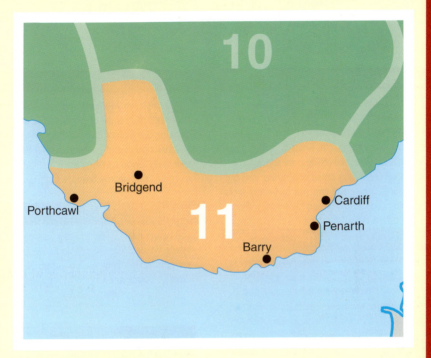

Cardiff is Wales's cosmopolitan capital city. It's a place of culture and the arts, with fine museums and theatres. It's also a city of great style – Cardiff's neoclassical civic architecture has won praise worldwide while the lavish city-centre castle, a seriously Victorian creation, never fails to astonish. The castle was built with the wealth generated by Cardiff's booming 19th-century seaport. The city is now renewing its maritime links through the exciting Cardiff Bay development, which is transforming the old waterfront. Close to the city there's attractive coast and countryside. The pastoral Vale of Glamorgan is dotted with picturesque villages and thatched cottages. And along the shore there's everything from the spectacular cliffs of the Glamorgan Heritage Coast to the popular resorts of Barry Island and Porthcawl.

It's a fact...

Cardiff was declared capital city of Wales in 1955. Its Victorian castle is built on the site of a 2000-year-old Roman fort. The Cardiff Bay development will create 8 miles of new waterfront and a 202-hectare/500-acre freshwater lake. Cardiff is only 2 hours by train from London. Cardiff-born author Roald Dahl was baptised in the city's Norwegian Church. The Glamorgan Heritage Coast, designated in 1973, runs for 14 miles between Aberthaw and Porthcawl. Merthyr Mawr has the highest sand dunes in Britain, rising to over 61m/200ft.

Cardiff and the Glamorgan Heritage Coast

Ma6   Barry/Barry Island

Town on narrow peninsula near Cardiff. Neighbouring Barry Island, with its sandy beaches, pleasure park and range of amusements, is a great favourite with fun seekers. The Knap, in contrast, has a quiet pebble beach, swimming pool and boating lake. Sports centre, sailing, bowls and fishing. Visit the Welsh Hawking Centre and two nearby beauty spots – Porthkerry Country Park and Dyffryn Gardens.

Mb5   Cardiff

Capital of Wales, business, trade and entertainment centre. Splendid Civic Centre, lovely parkland, modern pedestrianised shopping centre, new waterfront development, good restaurants, theatres, cinemas, clubs and sports facilities, including ice-rink and Superbowl. Visit St David's Hall for top-class entertainment. Ornate city-centre castle. National Museum and Gallery has a fine collection of Impressionist paintings. Industrial and Maritime Museum and Techniquest science discovery centre on Cardiff Bay waterfront. National Stadium is home of Welsh rugby. Llandaff Cathedral close by and fascinating collection of old farmhouses and other buildings at the Museum of Welsh Life St Fagans.

Le6   Cowbridge

Picturesque town with wide main street and pretty houses – the centre of the Vale of Glamorgan farming community. Fine old inns, shops selling high-class clothes and country wares. 14th-century town walls. Good touring centre for South Wales. Visit nearby Beaupre Castle.

Mb6   Penarth

Small resort near Cardiff offering boating, yachting, fishing, water-skiing and cliff walks. Victorian pier and promenade. New marina. Turner House Art Gallery. Cosmeston Country Park and Medieval Village nearby.

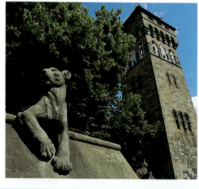

Penarth's promenade and pier

Cardiff Castle's clocktower (top)

74

Barry   Cardiff

SC | Flat 5

Heol-y-Gaer,
The Knap, Barry
Enquiries to: Mrs H.E. Cooper
3 Porth-y-Castell,
Barry CF62 6QA
Tel: (01446) 733784

Attractive, modern, fully furnished flat. Quiet residential area overlooking Bristol Channel, beach, gardens and lake. Ideally situated for shopping, sightseeing and nearby beautiful parks. Convenient for visiting picturesque villages and coastline of the Vale of Glamorgan.

		PER WEEK		SLEEPS
P	🐕			4 + COT
h	SP	MIN £	MAX £	
		185.00	210.00	FLAT	UNITS
		OPEN 1 - 12		1

SC | Pitman Cottage & Dogo Street

Pontcanna, Cardiff
Enquiries to: Mr C.A. Hooper
Kingsland, St Mary Church,
Cowbridge, CF71 7LT
Tel: (01446) 772773
Fax: (01222) 578281

Situated in residential area, easy walking distance to the city centre, close to sports centre, shops, restaurants and park. Comfortable, attractive accommodation providing all facilities for a pleasant stay in the capital city of Wales and as a base to explore the surrounding area. Easy and convenient road and rail access.

		PER WEEK		SLEEPS
P	h			4
SP	M	MIN £	MAX £	FLATS
📖		190.00	220.00	COTTAGE	UNITS
		OPEN 1 - 12		3

Pets welcome

You'll see from the symbols that many places to stay welcome dogs and pets by prior arrangement. Although some sections of beach may have restrictions, there are always adjacent areas – the promenade, for example, or quieter stretches of sands – where dogs can be exercised on and sometimes off leads. Please ask at a Tourist Information Centre for advice.

CP | Fontygary Holiday & Leisure Park

Fontygary Parks
Rhoose, nr Barry
CF62 3ZN
Tel: (01446) 710386
Fax: (01446) 710613

Fontygary Park is situated twelve miles from Cardiff. An ideal base to tour South and West Wales, easy access from M4. Superb facilities on park for all ages, including indoor swimming pool, family bars, entertainment, mini market and health club. All caravans fully equipped with colour TVs and microwave ovens. Pets welcome.

		PER WEEK	No. OF CARAVANS	
🐕			STATIC	HIRING
	✕	MIN £	MAX £	410	50
	🎵	80.00	360.00		
		OPEN 3 - 10		

DRAGON AWARD

The Dragon Award is your guide to the very best in individual caravan accommodation.

Award-winning caravans are extremely comfortable and luxuriously equipped – they include colour TV, heating and hot and cold water at no extra charge. Look out for the Dragon Award logo.

Dyffryn Gardens, Vale of Glamorgan

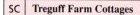

Cowbridge   Penarth

SC | Primrose Cottages

Church St, Wick,
Nr Cowbridge
Enquiries to: Mr Nicholls
Lamb & Flag Inn,
Church St,
Wick, Nr Cowbridge CF7 7QB
Tel: (01656) 890278

Primrose, Bluebell, Lamb, three delightful olde worlde cottages on the edge of the Glamorgan Heritage Coast. Each tastefully carpeted and furnished with television, modern kitchen, central heating, shower, toilet, free private parking. Near airport, Cardiff, Swansea, local beaches. Brochure on request.

P	h	PER WEEK			SLEEPS
SP	M	MIN £	MAX £	COTTAGES	4, 5, 5
		120.00	240.00		UNITS
		OPEN 1 - 12			3

SC | Treguff Farm Cottages

St Mary Church
Cowbridge
CF7 7LT
Tel: (01446) 751342 or
(01600) 860350

Stone cottages converted from a group of farm buildings adjacent to an Elizabethan farmhouse on a four hundred acre working stock farm. Specimen carp fishing available on farm lake. The interiors of the cottages have sympathetically retained most of the original architectural features. Excellent touring centre.

P	h	PER WEEK			SLEEPS
h		MIN £	MAX £	COTTAGES	2 - 8
		200.00	400.00		UNITS
		OPEN 1 - 12			4

SC | Lavernock Point Holiday Estate

Lavernock Point,
Fort Rd,
Penarth,
CF64 5XQ
Tel: (01222) 707310
Fax: (01222) 707310

Beautiful holiday village, just five miles away from central Cardiff. Consisting of privately owned self-catering holiday bungalows. Facilities include large outdoor heated swimming pool, clubhouse serving bar meals, laundry etc. Panoramic views overlooking the Bristol Channel and vast countryside landscapes. Ideal for as much action you want or rest you may need.

P	h	PER WEEK			SLEEPS
M		MIN £	MAX £	BUNGALOWS	4 - 6
		100.00	220.00	CHALETS	UNITS
		OPEN 3 - 12			30

CP | The Bay Caravan Park

St Mary's Well Bay,
Lavernock,
Penarth, CF64 5XS
Tel: (01222) 707512
Fax: (01222) 701975

A unique caravan park set in idyllic surroundings with private beach and panoramic views across the Bristol Channel. facilities include caravan and chalet accommodation, shop, launderette, amenities buildings, children's paddling pool, indoor heated swimming pool, tennis courts and modular designed children's play area. Everything to make the holiday a success.

		PER WEEK		No. OF CARAVANS	
		MIN £	MAX £	STATIC	HIRING
		80.00	285.00	219	11
				OPEN 3 - 10	

River Thaw, near Llanblethian

These two lovely valleys, close to the border, serve as the best possible introduction to Wales. The thickly wooded Wye Valley snakes its way northwards from Chepstow through countryside which is beautiful in all seasons. It's a walker's paradise, with a wonderful choice of trails including woodland, riverside and Offa's Dyke paths. Rolling green hills separate the Wye from the Usk, another beautiful river valley which reaches the sea at Newport. Fishermen, as well as walkers, love this part of Wales, for both rivers are famed for their salmon and trout. These borderlands, a natural gateway into Wales over the centuries, are dotted with historic sites of great significance – the Roman town of Caerleon, castles at almost every turn, and the splendid 17th-century mansion of Tredegar House, Newport.

It's a fact...

The **Wye Valley** between **Chepstow** and **Monmouth** is an 'Area of Outstanding Natural Beauty', designated in 1971. Britain's first stone-built castle was constructed at **Chepstow** in 1067. Charles Stewart Rolls, of Rolls-Royce celebrity, is a famous son of **Monmouth** – his statue stands in the town square. The majestic ruin of Tintern Abbey was founded in 1131 by Cistercian monks. The floral town of **Usk** is a regular 'Wales in Bloom' winner. Monmouth's fortified **Monnow Bridge** is the only one of its kind in Britain.

Mc1 Abergavenny

Flourishing market town with backdrop of mountains at south-eastern gateway to Brecon Beacons National Park. Pony trekking in nearby Black Mountains. Castle, Museum of Childhood and Home. Leisure centre. Monmouthshire and Brecon Canal runs just to the west of the town. Excellent touring base for the lovely Vale of Usk and Brecon Beacons.

Md3 Usk

Ancient borough on River Usk; excellent salmon fishing and inns. Good walks. Rural Life Museum, grass skiing. Great castle of Raglan 5 miles north. Sailing and other watersports on nearby Llandegfedd reservoir. Good central location for sightseeing.

Usk

Me3 Chepstow

Attractive hilly town with substantial remains of a great stone castle – reputedly the first to be built in Britain – above the Wye. Fortified gate still stands in main street and medieval walls remain. Good shopping. Museum, Stuart Crystal Engraving Workshop. Sunday market, fine racecourse, excellent walks – beginning of the Wye Valley Walk and Offa's Dyke Path. Ideal for touring beautiful Wye Valley.

Prices

In this publication we go to great lengths to make sure that you have a clear, accurate idea of prices and facilities. It's all spelled out in the 'Prices' section – and remember to confirm everything when making your booking.

SC Llyweddrog

Llanwenarth Citra,
Abergavenny, NP7 7LA
Enquiries to: Mrs N.E. Smith,
Penygraig Farm,
Llanwenarth Citra,
Abergavenny, NP7 7LA
Tel: (01873) 853398

Stone built farmhouse, high on Sugar Loaf Mountain. Situated at boundary of enclosed farmland and National Trust owned mountainside. Ideal centre for exploring Brecon Beacons and South Wales Valleys. Modern kitchen/diner, lounge with open fire, partial central heating.

h M	PER WEEK		SLEEPS
	MIN £	MAX £	6
	150.00	280.00	FARMHOUSE
			UNITS
	OPEN 5 - 10		1

SC Nightingale Cottage

Sunny Bank Farm,
Devauden,
Chepstow
NP6 6NS
Tel: (01291) 650365

Set on hillside giving idyllic atmosphere in unspoilt countryside. Perfect for walking, wildlife watching. Set near Wye Valley an Area of Outstanding Natural Beauty, close to Royal Forest of Dean, Brecon Beacons National Park. Tastefully furnished on theme of birds and flowers, central heating, kitchen fully fitted. Ideal family holiday, sporting leisure facilities in area. Fishing nearby. Good views, peaceful, private only 2 minutes from road, shop, garage, pub nearby. Sheer tranquillity.

P h	PER WEEK		SLEEPS
SP M	MIN £	MAX £	6
	120.00	240.00	COTTAGE
			UNITS
	OPEN 3 - 1		1

SC The Pheasant Pens

Brace Farm,
LLandenny,
Nr Usk
NP5 1DN
Tel: (01291) 690216

Situated in beautiful countryside within easy reach of good walking country, the Wye Valley, Brecon Beacons and many historic towns. These two comfortable cottages, in converted farm buildings, are equipped to a very high standard including colour TV, video, microwave and laundry room. A warm welcome awaits all.

P	PER WEEK		SLEEPS
h SP	MIN £	MAX £	2 - 4
	140.00	350.00	COTTAGES
			UNITS
	OPEN 1 - 12		2

SCA	Coastal Cottages of Pembrokeshire

The Holiday
Information Centre,
No 2 Riverside Quay,
Haverfordwest
SA61 2LJ
Tel: (01437) 765765
Fax: (01437) 769900

Best in Wales - Award winning luxury cottages within the Pembrokeshire coast and Preseli Hills National Parks. Beautiful stone cottages and luxury modern houses chosen for their idyllic locations and exceptional quality. A free guide book and experienced staff help you choose your very special holiday.

P 🐕		PER WEEK	HOUSES	SLEEPS
h ▢		MIN £	MAX £	FARMHOUSES	2 - 12
SP	M	130.00	850.00	FLATS COTTAGES	UNITS
🔲		OPEN 1 - 12	BUNGALOWS	400

Journey Through Wales

Magnificently produced book, the ideal gift or memento. High quality photographs with accompanying text take you on a tour of Wales. Classic views of Wales's scenic mountains and coastline. A complete pictorial record – everything from powerful castles to colourful craft workshops, picturesque villages to narrow–gauge railways.

£4.80 inc. p&p

(see 'Guides and Maps' at the end of the book)

Please note

All the accommodation in this publication has applied for verification/classification and in many instances for grading also. However, at the time of going to press not all establishments had been visited – some of these properties are indicated by the wording 'Awaiting Inspection' or 'Awaiting Grading'.

WALES CYMRU
LAND OF INSPIRATION

Monkstone beach, Pembrokeshire

Make the most of your stay in Wales by contacting one of our Tourist Information Centres for help on all aspects of your holiday. TIC staff will be delighted to assist with:

- booking your accommodation *(see below)* • places to visit • places to eat • things to do
- routes to take • national and local events • maps, guides and books

Tourist Information Centres

Normal opening times are 10am–3pm. These hours may vary to suit local circumstances. Those marked with an asterisk (*) are open seasonally only (April–September).

The Bed Booking Service is free for local reservations. A £1 fee applies to bookings made further afield in Wales.

Aberaeron	The Quay, Aberaeron SA46 0BT	Tel (01545) 570602
Aberdovey / Aberdyfi *	Wharf Gardens, Aberdovey LL35 0ED	Tel (01654) 767321
Abergavenny *	Swan Meadow, Monmouth Road, Abergavenny NP7 5HH	Tel (01873) 857588
Aberystwyth	Terrace Road, Aberystwyth SY23 2AG	Tel (01970) 612125
Bala	Penllyn, Pensarn Road, Bala LL23 7SR	Tel (01678) 521021
Bangor *	Little Chef Services, A55/A5 Llandygai, Bangor LL57 7BG	Tel (01248) 352786
Barmouth *	Old Library, Station Road, Barmouth LL42 1LU	Tel (01341) 280787
Barry Island *	The Triangle, Paget Road, Barry Island CF62 8TJ	Tel (01446) 747171
Betws-y-Coed	Royal Oak Stables, Betws-y-Coed LL24 0AH	Tel (01690) 710426
Blaenau Ffestiniog *	Isallt, High Street, Blaenau Ffestiniog LL41 3HD	Tel (01766) 830360
Borth *	High Street, The Promenade, Borth SY24 5HY	Tel (01970) 871174
Brecon	Cattle Market Car Park, Brecon LD3 9DA	Tel (01874) 622485
Builth Wells	Groe Car Park, Builth Wells LD2 3BT	Tel (01982) 553307
Caerleon	High Street, Caerleon	Tel (01633) 422656
Caernarfon	Oriel Pendeitsh, Castle Street, Caernarfon LL55 2NA	Tel (01286) 672232
Caerphilly	Twyn Square, Caerphilly	Tel (01222) 851378
Cardiff	Central Station, Cardiff CF1 1QY	Tel (01222) 227281
Cardigan	Theatr Mwldan, Bath House Road, Cardigan SA43 2JY	Tel (01239) 613230
Carmarthen	Lammas Street, Carmarthen SA31 3AQ	Tel (01267) 231557
Chepstow	Castle Car Park, Bridge Street, Chepstow NP6 5EY	Tel (01291) 623772
Colwyn Bay	40 Station Road, Colwyn Bay LL29 8BU	Tel (01492) 530478
Conwy	Conwy Castle Visitor Centre, Conwy LL32 8LD	Tel (01492) 592248
Corris *	Craft Centre, Corris, nr Machynlleth SY20 9SP	Tel (01654) 761244
Crickhowell *	Beaufort Chambers, Beaufort Street, Crickhowell NP8 1AA	Tel (01873) 812105
Cwmcarn	Visitor Centre, Cwmcarn Forest Drive, nr Cross Keys NP1 7FA	Tel (01495) 272001
Dolgellau	Tŷ Meirion, Eldon Square, Dolgellau LL40 1PU	Tel (01341) 422888
Elan Valley *	Elan Valley Visitor Centre, Elan Valley, nr Rhayader LD6 5HP	Tel (01597) 810898
Ewloe	Autolodge Services, A55 Westbound, Northophall, Ewloe CH7 6HE	Tel (01244) 541597
Fishguard Harbour	Passenger Concourse, The Harbour, Goodwick, Fishguard SA64 0BU	Tel (01348) 872037
Fishguard Town	4 Hamilton Street, Fishguard SA65 9HL	Tel (01348) 873484
Harlech *	Gwyddfor House, High Street, Harlech LL46 2YA	Tel (01766) 780658
Haverfordwest	Old Bridge, Haverfordwest SA61 2EZ	Tel (01437) 763110
Holyhead	Marine Square, Salt Island Approach, Holyhead LL65 1DR	Tel (01407) 762622
Kilgetty *	Kingsmoor Common, Kilgetty SA68 0YA	Tel (01834) 813672
Knighton	Offa's Dyke Centre, West Street, Knighton LD7 1EW	Tel (01547) 528753
Lake Vyrnwy	Unit 2, Vyrnwy Craft Workshops, Lake Vyrnwy SY10 0LY	Tel (01691) 870346
Llanberis *	41 High Street, Llanberis	Tel (01286) 870765
Llandarcy *	BP Club, Llandarcy, Neath SA10 6HJ	Tel (01792) 813030
Llandovery *	Central Car Park, Broad Street, Llandovery SA20 0AR	Tel (01550) 720693

Llandrindod Wells	Old Town Hall, Memorial Gardens, Llandrindod Wells LD1 5DL	Tel (01597) 822600
Llandudno	1-2 Chapel Street, Llandudno LL30 2YU	Tel (01492) 876413
Llanelli	Public Library, Vaughan Street, Llanelli SA15 3AS	Tel (01554) 772020
Llanfairpwllgwyngyll	Station Site, Llanfairpwllgwyngyll LL61 5UJ	Tel (01248) 713177
Llangollen	Town Hall, Castle Street, Llangollen LL20 5PD	Tel (01978) 860828
Llanidloes	Town Hall, Great Oak Street, Llanidloes SY18 6BN	Tel (01686) 412605
Llanwrtyd Wells	Tŷ Barcud, The Square, Llanwrtyd Wells LD5 4RB	Tel (01591) 610666
Machynlleth	Canolfan Owain Glyndŵr, Machynlleth SY20 8EE	Tel (01654) 702401
Magor	Granada Services West, Junction 23 M4, Magor NP6 3YL	Tel (01633) 881122
Merthyr Tydfil	14a Glebeland Street, Merthyr Tydfil CF47 8AU	Tel (01685) 379884
Milford Haven *	94 Charles Street, Milford Haven SA73 2HL	Tel (01646) 690866
Mold	Library, Museum and Art Gallery, Earl Road, Mold CH7 1AP	Tel (01352) 759331
Monmouth *	Shire Hall, Agincourt Square, Monmouth NP5 3DY	Tel (01600) 713899
Mumbles *	Oystermouth Square, Mumbles, Swansea SA3 4DQ	Tel (01792) 361302
Narberth	Town Hall, Narberth SA67 7AR	Tel (01834) 860061
New Quay *	Church Street, New Quay SA45 9NZ	Tel (01545) 560865
Newcastle Emlyn *	Market Hall, Newcastle Emlyn SA38 9AE	Tel (01239) 711333
Newport	Newport Museum & Art Gallery, John Frost Square, Newport NP9 1HZ	Tel (01633) 842962
Newtown	Central Car Park, Newtown SY16 2PW	Tel (01686) 625580
Pembroke	Visitor Centre, Commons Road, Pembroke SA71 4EA	Tel (01646) 622388
Pembroke Dock *	Guntower, Front Street	Tel (01646) 622246
Penarth *	Penarth Pier, The Esplanade, Penarth CF64 3AU	Tel (01222) 708849
Pont Abraham	Pont Abraham Services, Junction 49 M4, Llanedi SA4 1FP	Tel (01792) 883838
Pontardawe	3 Herbert Street, Pontardawe	Tel (01792) 864475
Pont Nedd Fechan	nr Glyn Neath SA11 5NR	Tel (01639) 721795
Pontypridd	Historical and Cultural Centre, The Old Bridge, Pontypridd CF37 3PE	Tel (01443) 409512
Porthcawl	Old Police Station, John Street, Porthcawl CF36 3DT	Tel (01656) 786639
Porthmadog	High Street, Porthmadog LL49 9LP	Tel (01766) 512981
Prestatyn *	Scala Cinema, High Street, Prestatyn LL19 9LH	Tel (01745) 889092
Presteigne *	Old Market Hall, Broad Street, Presteigne LD8 2AW	Tel (01544) 260193
Pwllheli	Min y Don, Station Square, Pwllheli LL53 5HG	Tel (01758) 613000
Rhayader	Leisure Centre, Rhayader LD6 5BU	Tel (01597) 810591
Rhos on Sea *	The Promenade, Rhos on Sea LL28 4EP	Tel (01492) 548778
Rhyl	Rhyl Children's Village, West Parade, Rhyl LL18 1HZ	Tel (01745) 355068
Ruthin	Ruthin Craft Centre, Park Road, Ruthin LL15 1BB	Tel (01824) 703992
St David's *	City Hall, St David's SA62 6SD	Tel (01437) 720392
Sarn	Sarn Park Services, Junction 36 M4, nr Bridgend CF32 9SY	Tel (01656) 654906
Swansea	PO Box 59, Singleton Street, Swansea SA1 3QG	Tel (01792) 468321
Tenby	The Croft, Tenby SA70 8AP	Tel (01834) 842402
Tregaron	The Square, Tregaron SY25 6JN	Tel (01974) 298144
Tywyn *	High Street, Tywyn LL36 9AD	Tel (01654) 710070
Welshpool	Flash Leisure Centre, Salop Road, Welshpool SY21 7DH	Tel (01938) 552043
Wrexham	Lambpit Street, Wrexham LL11 1AY	Tel (01978) 292015

And at Oswestry on the Wales/England border

Heritage Centre	2 Church Terrace, Oswestry SY11 2TE	Tel (01691) 662753
Mile End Services	Oswestry SY11 4JA	Tel (01691) 662488

Wales in London's West End

If you're in London, call in at the Wales Information Bureau, British Travel Centre, 12 Lower Regent Street, Piccadilly Circus, London SW1Y 4PQ. Tel (0171) 409 0969. Staff there will give you all the information you need to plan your visit to Wales.

Further Information

Travel facts

By rail

Please contact your local travel agent or principal stations:

Birmingham – Tel (0121) 643 2711

Cardiff – Tel (01222) 228000

London (to North Wales) – Tel (0171) 387 7070

London (to South Wales) – Tel (0171) 262 6767

Manchester – Tel (0161) 832 8353

There are eight members of Wales's narrow-gauge 'Great Little Trains': Bala Lake Railway, Brecon Mountain Railway (Merthyr Tydfil), Ffestiniog Railway (Porthmadog), Llanberis Lake Railway, Talyllyn Railway (Tywyn), Vale of Rheidol Railway (Aberystwyth), Welsh Highland Railway (Porthmadog) and Welshpool and Llanfair Railway (Llanfair Caereinion). 'Great Little Trains' details are available from The Station, Llanfair Caereinion SY21 0SF (tel 01938-810441).

The railways operating independently of 'Great Little Trains' are: Fairbourne and Barmouth Steam Railway (tel 01341-250362), Gwili Railway, nr Carmarthen (tel 01267-230666), Llangollen Railway (tel 01978-860951), Snowdon Mountain Railway, Llanberis (tel 01286-870223) and Teifi Valley Railway, nr Newcastle Emlyn (tel 01559-371077).

By coach

Contact your local travel agent or National Express office. For all National Express enquiries please telephone the Nationalcall number (0990) 808080 (calls cost a maximum of 10p per minute, less at off-peak times).

By sea

Five services operate across the Irish Sea:

Cork to Swansea (Swansea-Cork Ferries, tel 01792-456116)

Dublin to Holyhead (Irish Ferries, tel 0151-227 3131)

Dun Laoghaire to Holyhead (Stena Sealink – a choice of three services: High-Speed Superferry, tel 01233-615455, Sea Lynx Catamaran, tel 01233-647047, and Ferry, tel 01233-647047)

Rosslare to Fishguard (Stena Sealink – a choice of two services: Sea Lynx Catamaran and Ferry, tel 01233-647047)

Rosslare to Pembroke Dock (Irish Ferries, tel 0151-227 3132)

By air

There are direct flights from Aberdeen, Amsterdam, Belfast, Brussels, Channel Islands, Dublin, Edinburgh, Glasgow, Isle of Man, Manchester and Paris to Cardiff International Airport (tel 01446-711111), 12 miles from the city centre. Connecting services worldwide are via Amsterdam. Manchester and Birmingham Airports are also convenient gateways for Wales.

Gwyliau Cymru/ Festivals of Wales

This is the collective voice for over 50 arts festivals, embracing everything from classical music to jazz, children's events to drama. *For more information, please contact:* Festivals of Wales, Red House, Newtown SY16 3LE Tel (01686) 626442

The following organisations and authorities will be pleased to provide any further information you require when planning your holiday to Wales.

Wales Tourist Board, Dept SCG, Davis Street, Cardiff CF1 2FU Tel (01222) 475226

(Holiday and travel information is available from the above address, together with a free leaflet explaining the WTB's 'Quest for Quality' inspection schemes.)

Holiday information is also available from:

North Wales Tourism, Dept SCG, 77 Conway Road, Colwyn Bay LL29 7BL Tel (01492) 531731 Holiday Bookings (0800) 834820

Mid Wales Tourism, Dept SCG, The Station, Machynlleth SY20 8TG Tel (01654) 702653 Holiday Bookings (0800) 273747

Tourism South and West Wales, Dept SCG, Charter Court, Enterprise Park, Swansea SA7 9DB Tel (01792) 781212 (quote Dept SCG) Holiday Bookings (0800) 243731

Tourism South and West Wales, Dept SCG, Old Bridge, Haverfordwest, Pembrokeshire SA62 2EZ Tel (01437) 766330 (quote Dept SCG) Holiday Bookings (0800) 243731

Wales on the Internet

A wide range of travel and holiday information on Wales is now available on the Wales Tourist Board's Internet address:

www.tourism.wales.gov.uk

Other useful addresses

Brecon Beacons National Park,
Park Office, 7 Glamorgan Street,
Brecon LD3 7DP
Tel (01874) 624437

Cadw: Welsh Historic Monuments,
Brunel House, 2 Fitzalan Road,
Cardiff CF2 1UY
Tel (01222) 465511

Football Association of Wales,
3 Westgate Street, Cardiff CF1 1DD
Tel (01222) 372325

Forestry Enterprise (Forestry Commission),
Victoria House, Victoria Terrace,
Aberystwyth SY23 2DQ
Tel (01970) 612367

National Trust,
North Wales Regional Office,
Trinity Square,
Llandudno LL30 2DE
Tel (01492) 860123

National Trust,
South Wales Regional Office,
The King's Head, Bridge Street,
Llandeilo SA19 6BB
Tel (01558) 822800

National Rivers Authority,
(Fisheries and Conservation
enquiries), Plas-yr-Afon,
St Mellons Business Park,
St Mellons, Cardiff CF3 0LT
Tel (01222) 770088

Offa's Dyke Centre,
West Street, Knighton LD7 1EN
Tel (01547) 528753

Pembrokeshire Coast National Park,
National Park Department,
County Offices, St Thomas Green,
Haverfordwest SA61 1QZ
Tel (01437) 764591

Ramblers' Association in Wales,
Ty'r Cerddwyr, High Street,
Gresford, Wrexham LL12 8PT
Tel (01978) 855148

Snowdonia National Park,
Snowdonia National Park Office,
Penrhyndeudraeth LL48 6LS
Tel (01766) 770274

Surfcall Wales
(daily surf/weather conditions at
all major beaches)
Tel (0839) 505697/360361
Calls cost 39p per minute cheap
rate, 49p per minute at all other
times

Taste of Wales-*Blas ar Gymru,*
Welsh Food Promotions Ltd,
Cardiff Business Technology
Centre, Senghenydd Road,
Cardiff CF2 4AY
Tel (01222) 640456

Wales Craft Council,
Park Lane House, 7 High Street,
Welshpool SY21 7JP
Tel (01938) 555313

Welsh Golfing Union,
Catsash, Newport NP6 1JQ
Tel (01633) 430830

Welsh Rugby Union,
Cardiff Arms Park, PO Box 22,
Cardiff CF1 1JL
Tel (01222) 390111

Youth Hostels Association,
1 Cathedral Road,
Cardiff CF1 9HA
Tel (01222) 396766

We'll show you around

The Wales Official Tourist Guides
offer an expert guiding service at
very reasonable fees – from
hourly tours by car or coach to
extended tours of any duration
throughout Wales. WOTG guides
and driver/guides are the only
qualified tourist guides in Wales,
and the association is registered
with the Wales Tourist Board.
Further details from:
Derek Jones,
Y Stabl, 30 Acton Gardens,
Box Lane, Wrexham LL12 8DE
Tel (01978) 351212
Fax (01978) 363060

Information for visitors with disabilities

The wheelchair accessibility
guidelines in the 'Where to Stay'
sections of this publication are
designed to provide reliable and
consistent information through
standardised inspection schemes.
All properties in this book
identified as being accessible to
disabled visitors have been
inspected by the Wales Tourist
Board.

Discovering Accessible Wales is an
information-packed guide for
visitors who may have impaired
movement or are confined to a
wheelchair. The book is available
free from the Wales Tourist Board.
See 'Guides and Maps' at the end
of this publication for details.

For details of other wheelchair-
accessible accommodation
inspected to the same standards
please contact the Holiday Care
Service. This organisation also
provides a wide range of other
travel and holiday information
for disabled visitors:

Holiday Care Service,
2nd Floor, Imperial Buildings,
Victoria Road, Horley,
Surrey RH6 7PZ
Tel (01293) 774535

Other helpful organisations

Wales Council for the Blind,
Shand House, 20 Newport Road,
Cardiff CF2 1DB
Tel (01222) 473954

Wales Council for the Deaf,
Maritime Offices,
Woodland Terrace, Maes-y-Coed,
Pontypridd CF37 1DZ
Tel (01443) 485687
Minicom (01443) 485686

Disability Wales,
Llys Ifor, Crescent Road,
Caerphilly CF83 1XL
Tel (01222) 887325/6/7/8

Trespass – a word of warning
If you're out and about enjoying
an activity holiday – walking off
established footpaths, mountain
biking, or even landing your
paraglider! – please obtain
permission from landowners. To
avoid any problems, it's always
best to seek out the appropriate
permission beforehand.

British Tourist Authority Overseas Offices

Your enquiries will be welcome at the offices of the British Tourist Authority in the following countries:

ARGENTINA
British Tourist Authority, 2nd Floor,
Avenida Cordoba 645,
1054 Buenos Aires
(open to the public 1000-1400 only)
Tel (1) 314 5514   Fax(1) 314 8955

AUSTRALIA
British Tourist Authority, 8th Floor,
University Centre, 210 Clarence Street,
Sydney, NSW 2000
Tel (2) 261 607   Fax (2) 267 4442

BELGIUM
British Tourist Authority,
306 Avenue Louise,
1050 Brussels
Tel (2) 646 35 10   Fax (2) 646 39 86

CANADA
British Tourist Authority,
111 Avenue Road,
Suite 450, Toronto, Ontario M5R 3J8
Tel (416) 925 6326   Fax (416) 961 2175

CZECH AND SLOVAK REPUBLICS
British Tourist Authority, Kaprova 13,
110 01 Prague 1, PO Box 264
Tel (2) 232 7213   Fax (2) 232 7469

DENMARK
British Tourist Authority, Montergade 3,
1116 Copenhagen K
Tel 33 91 88

FRANCE
Tourisme de Grande-Bretagne,
Maison de la Grande-Bretagne,
19 rue des Mathurins, 75009 Paris
(entre les rues Tronchet et Auber)
Tel 44 51 56 20   Fax 44 51 56 21
Minitel 3615 BRITISH

GERMANY
British Tourist Authority,
Taunusstrasse 52-60,
60329 Frankfurt
Tel (69) 2380711   Fax (69) 2380717

GREECE
Action Public Relations, Kritonos 23,
Pangratu, GR 161-21
Tel (1) 72 40 160   Fax (1) 72 23 417

HONG KONG
British Tourist Authority, Room 1504,
Eton Tower, 8 Hysan Avenue,
Causeway Bay, Hong Kong
Tel 2882 9967   Fax 2577 1443

IRELAND
British Tourist Authority,
18-19 College Green, Dublin 2
Tel (1) 670 8000   Fax (1) 670 8244

ITALY
British Tourist Authority,
Corso V. Emanuele 337,
00186 Rome
Tel (6) 68806464   Fax (6) 6879095
(solo ricezione)

JAPAN
British Tourist Authority,
Tokyo Club Building,
3-2-6 Kasumigaseki, Chiyoda-ku,
Tokyo 100
Tel (3) 3581 3603/4   Fax (3) 3581 5797

NETHERLANDS
British Tourist Authority,
Aurora Gebouw (5e),
Stadhouderskade 2, 1054 ES Amsterdam
Tel (2) 685 50 51

NEW ZEALAND
British Tourist Authority, Suite 305,
3rd Floor, Dilworth Building,
corner Queen and Customs Streets,
Auckland 1
Tel (9) 303 1446   Fax (9) 377 6965

NORWAY
British Tourist Authority,
Nedre Slotts Gt 21,
4 etasje, N-0157 Oslo
Tel (2) 424 745
(as soon as you hear voice, press 200)
Postbox 1554 Vika, N-0117 Oslo

SINGAPORE
British Tourist Authority,
24 Raffles Place,
#19-06 Clifford Centre, Singapore 0104
Tel 535 2966   Fax 534 4703

SOUTH AFRICA
British Tourist Authority,
Lancaster Gate,
Hyde Lane, Hyde Park,
Sandton 2196 *(visitors)*
PO Box 41896, Craighall 2024
(postal address)
Tel (11) 325 0343

SPAIN
British Tourist Authority,
Torre de Madrid 6/5,
Plaza de Espana 18, 28008, Madrid
Tel (1) 541 13 96   Fax (1) 542 81 49

SWEDEN
British Tourist Authority, Klara Norra,
Kyrkogata 29,
S 111 22 Stockholm *(visitors)*
Box 745, S 101 35 Stockholm
(postal address)
Tel (8) 21 24 44   Fax (8) 21 31 29

SWITZERLAND
British Tourist Authority,
Limmatquai 78, CH-8001 Zurich
Tel (1) 261 42 77   Fax (1) 251 44 56

USA
CHICAGO
British Tourist Authority,
625 N Michigan Avenue, Suite 1510,
Chicago IL 60611 *(personal callers only)*

NEW YORK
British Tourist Authority,
551 Fifth Avenue, New York,
NY 10176-0799
Tel 1 800 GO 2 BRITAIN
Fax (212) 986 1188

A Brief Guide to the Welsh Language

A few greetings

Welsh	English
Bore da	Good morning
Dydd da	Good day
Prynhawn da	Good afternoon
Noswaith dda	Good evening
Nos da	Good night
Sut mae?	How are you?
Hwyl	Cheers
Diolch	Thanks
Diolch yn fawr iawn	Thanks very much
Croeso	Welcome
Croeso i Gymru	Welcome to Wales
Da	Good
Da iawn	Very good
Iechyd da!	Good health!
Nadolig Llawen!	Merry Christmas!
Blwyddyn Newydd Dda!	Happy New Year!
Dymuniadau gorau	Best wishes
Cyfarchion	Greetings
Penblwydd hapus	Happy birthday

The Welsh National Anthem

Mae hen wlad fy nhadau yn annwyl i mi,
Gwlad beirdd a chantorion enwogion o fri;
Ei gwrol ryfelwyr, gwladgarwyr tra mad,
Dros ryddid collasant eu gwaed.

Chorus
Gwlad! Gwlad! Pleidiol wyf i'm gwlad;
Tra môr yn fur i'r bur hoff bau,
O bydded i'r hen iaith barhau.

The ancient land of my fathers is dear to me,
A land of poets and minstrels, famed men.
Her brave warriors, patriots much blessed,
It was for freedom that they lost their blood.

Chorus
Homeland! I am devoted to my country;
So long as the sea is a wall to this fair beautiful land,
May the ancient language remain.

Pronunciation

There are some sounds in spoken Welsh which are very different from their English equivalents. Here's a basic guide.

Welsh		English equivalent
c	**c**ath *(cat)*	**c**at (never as in re**c**eive)
ch	**ch**waer *(sister)*	lo**ch**
dd	yn **dd**a *(good)*	**th**em
f	y **f**am *(the mother)*	o**f**
ff	**ff**enestr *(window)*	o**ff**
g	**g**ardd *(garden)*	**g**arden (never as in **G**eorge)
h	**h**et *(hat)*	**h**at (never silent as in **h**onest)
th	by**th** *(ever)*	**Th**ree (never as in **th**e)
ll	**ll**aw *(hand)*	There is no equivalent

sound. Place the tongue on the upper roof of the mouth near the upper teeth, ready to pronounce **l**; then blow rather than voice the **l**

The vowels in Welsh are **a e i o u w y**; all except **y** can be l-o-n-g or short:

long **a**	*tad (father)*	similar to h**a**rd
short **a**	m**a**m *(mother)*	similar to h**a**m
long **e**	h**e**n *(old)*	similar to s**a**ne
short **e**	p**e**n *(head)*	similar to t**e**n
long **i**	m**i**s *(month)*	similar to g**ee**se
short **i**	pr**i**n *(scarce)*	similar to t**i**n
long **o**	m**ô**r *(sea)*	similar to m**o**re
short **o**	ff**o**n *(walking stick)*	similar to f**o**nd
long **w**	s**ŵ**n *(sound)*	similar to m**oo**n
short **w**	g**w**n *(gun)*	similar to l**oo**k

y has two sounds:

1. Clear
d**y**n *(man)* a long 'ee' sound almost like g**ee**se
c**y**n *(before)* a short 'i' sound almost like t**i**n

2. Obscure
something like the sound in English r**u**n, eg:
y *(the)*
yn *(in)*
d**y**nion *(men)*

It is well to remember that in Welsh the accent usually falls on the last syllable but one of a word, eg c**a**dair *(chair)*.

LLANFAIRPWLLGWYNGYLLGOGERYCHWYRNDROBWLLLLANTYSILIOGOGOGOCH

Llan-vire-pooll-guin-gill-go-ger-u-queern-drob-ooll-llandus-ilio-gogo-goch

Get Yourself a Guide

If you want more information or are still undecided on a place to stay, you'll find the answers in this extensive range of publications.

Wales – Self-Catering is one of a series of three official 1996 accommodation guides. All places listed have been checked out by the Wales Tourist Board. These full-colour guides also contain detailed maps and comprehensive tourist information.

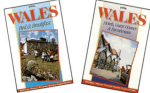

Wales - Hotels, Guest Houses & Farmhouses 1996 £2.95

A wide cross-section of accommodation, with a great choice of places to stay throughout Wales. Something for all tastes and pockets.

Wales - Bed and Breakfast 1996 £2.95

See Wales on a budget with this guide. Hundreds of hotels, guest houses and farmhouses, all with one thing in common – they offer B&B for £20 or under, per person per night.

Wales Tourist Map £2

A best-seller – and now better than ever. Detailed 5 miles/inch scale, fully revised and updated. Also includes suggested car tours, town plans, information centres.

A Journey Through Wales £4.80

A magnificent production – 64 big-format pages of the best images in Wales. The 90 photographs take the reader on a tour of Wales's mighty castles, spectacular mountains and coastline, country towns and colourful attractions.

Visitor's Guides to South, Mid and North Wales £3.55 each

Another series of best-sellers, written by Welsh author Roger Thomas. These three information-packed books give you the complete picture of Wales's holiday regions. In full colour – and fully updated.

- Descriptions of resorts, towns and villages
- Where to go and what to see
- Hundreds of attractions and places to visit
- Scenic drives, castles, crafts, what to do on a rainy day
- Detailed maps and town plans

Wales - Castles and Historic Places £7

Describes more than 140 sites in full colour, including castles, abbeys, country houses, prehistoric and Roman remains. A historic introduction sets the scene, and detailed maps help visitors plan their routes.

Wales - A Touring Guide to Crafts £6.80

Specially devised tours in full colour take you to galleries, woodcarvers, potters, jewellers and woollen mills. Nearly 100 craft workshops are listed, together with other places to visit.

'By Car' Guides   £2.30 each

- The Pembrokeshire Coast
- The Brecon Beacons

Two of the 32-page White Horse series. Attractive routes, maps and photographs – the ideal car touring guides to these beautiful parts of Wales.

Ordnance Survey Pathfinder Guides £8.45 each

- Snowdonia Walks (including Anglesey/Llŷn Peninsula)
- Pembrokeshire and Gower Walks
- Brecon Beacons and Glamorgan Walks

80-page books with detailed maps, colour illustrations and descriptions which guide you safely along attractive walking routes.

All prices include postage and packing

FREE PUBLICATIONS

Cycling Wales

See Wales on two wheels. A selection of cycling opportunities, from mountain biking to leisurely routes. Accommodation and cycle hire can be arranged with just one phone call through this brochure.

Discover Wales on Horseback

Full of information on trekking and riding, with a list of accredited centres located throughout Wales, many of which also offer accommodation.

Discovering Accessible Wales

A guide full of ideas and helpful information for people who may have impaired movement or are confined to a wheelchair. Covers everything from accommodation to activities. Available from March 1996.

Freedom Holiday Parks Wales

Caravan Holiday Home Park accommodation in Wales is high on standards and value for money – as you'll see from this brochure which only lists parks graded for quality by the Wales Tourist Board.

Golf in Wales

Beautifully produced large-format guide to Wales's golf courses in full colour, written by Peter Corrigan, Golf Correspondent of the *Independent on Sunday*.

Wales Arts Season '96

Attractive booklet on Wales's thriving and diverse arts scene, with information on events, festivals, theatres, galleries and museums. Available from March 1996.

Wales Touring Caravan and Camping

Detailed guide to Wales Tourist Board-inspected caravan and camping parks which welcome touring caravans, motorhomes and tents.

Walking Wales

A booklet on Britain's most popular leisure activity – and the best place in which to enjoy it. Suggested walks, lists of walking holiday operators and information on the countryside.

The Walled Towns of Wales and Chester

Fascinating 60-page colour guide to medieval walled towns, including Caernarfon, Conwy, Pembroke and Tenby. Historical sites plus tourist information.

PLEASE COMPLETE AND SEND TO: WALES TOURIST BOARD, DEPT SC96, DAVIS STREET, CARDIFF CF1 2FU

SALEABLE PUBLICATIONS

Please enclose the appropriate remittance in the form of a cheque (payable to Wales Tourist Board) or postal/money order in £ sterling. All prices include post and packing.

☐ Wales – Hotels, Guest Houses & Farm Houses 1996	£2.95	
☐ Wales – Self-Catering 1996	£2.95	
☐ Wales Tourist Map	£2	
☐ A Journey Through Wales	£4.80	
☐ A Visitor's Guide to South Wales	£3.55	
☐ A Visitor's Guide to Mid Wales	£3.55	
☐ A Visitor's Guide to North Wales	£3.55	
☐ Wales – Castles & Historic Places	£7	
☐ Wales – A Touring Guide to Crafts	£6.80	

OS Pathfinder Guides:

☐ Snowdonia Walks *(including Anglesey/Llŷn Peninsula)*	£8.45
☐ Pembrokeshire & Gower Walks	£8.45
☐ Brecon Beacons & Glamorgan Walks	£8.45

'By Car' Guides:

☐ The Pembrokeshire Coast	£2.30
☐ The Brecon Beacons	£2.30

FREE PUBLICATIONS

- ☐ Cycling Wales
- ☐ Discover Wales on Horseback
- ☐ Discovering Accessible Wales
- ☐ Freedom Holiday Parks Wales
- ☐ Golf in Wales
- ☐ Wales Arts Season '96
- ☐ Wales Touring Caravan & Camping
- ☐ Walking Wales
- ☐ The Walled Towns of Wales & Chester

Name *(please print)*: ....

Address *(please print)*: ....

....Post Code: ....

Total remittance enclosed *(if applicable)*: £ ....   Cheque *(payable to Wales Tourist Board)* /PO or Money Order No *(if applicable)*:.............................

Maps of Wales

The maps which follow divide Wales into 12 sections, each with a slight overlap. The grid overlaying each map will help you find the resort, town or village of your choice. Please refer to the map and grid reference which appears alongside the name of each place listed in the 'Where to Stay' gazetteers.

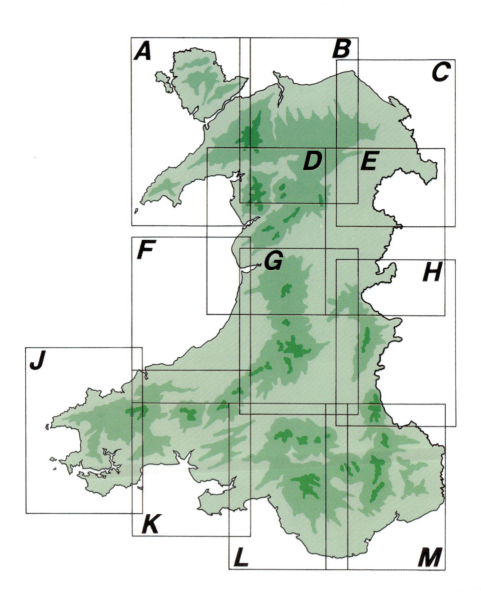

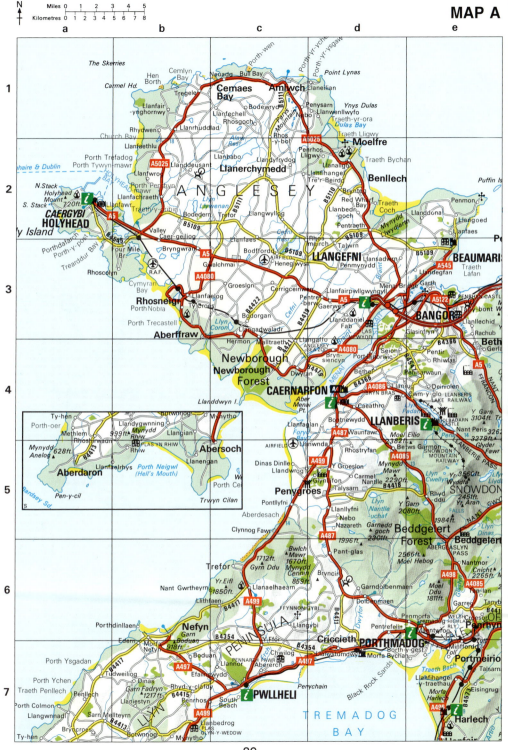

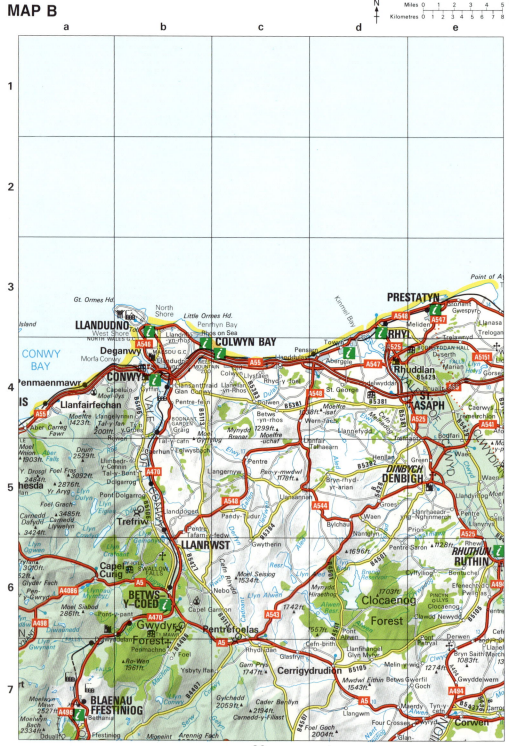

MAP B

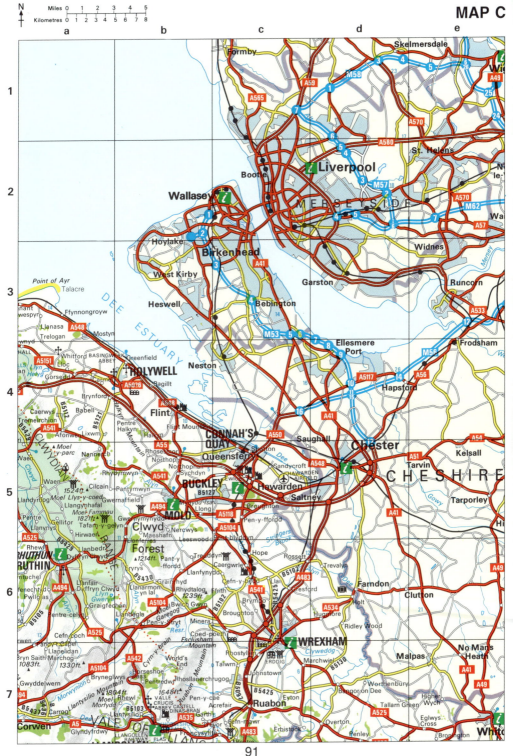

MAP C

MAP D

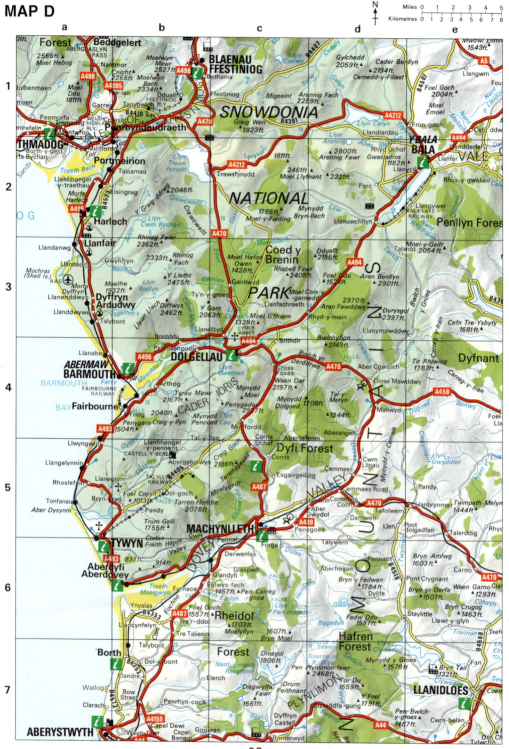

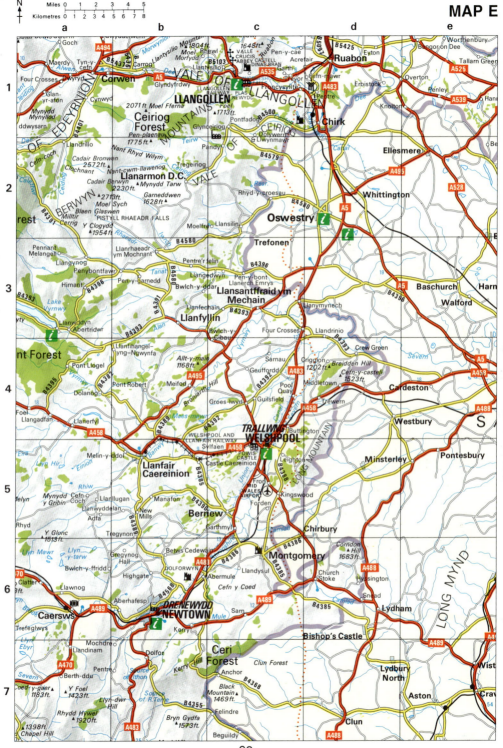

MAP F

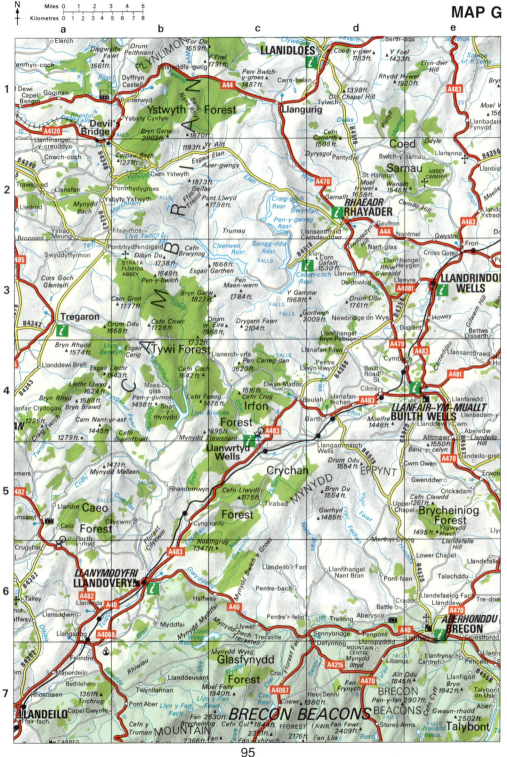

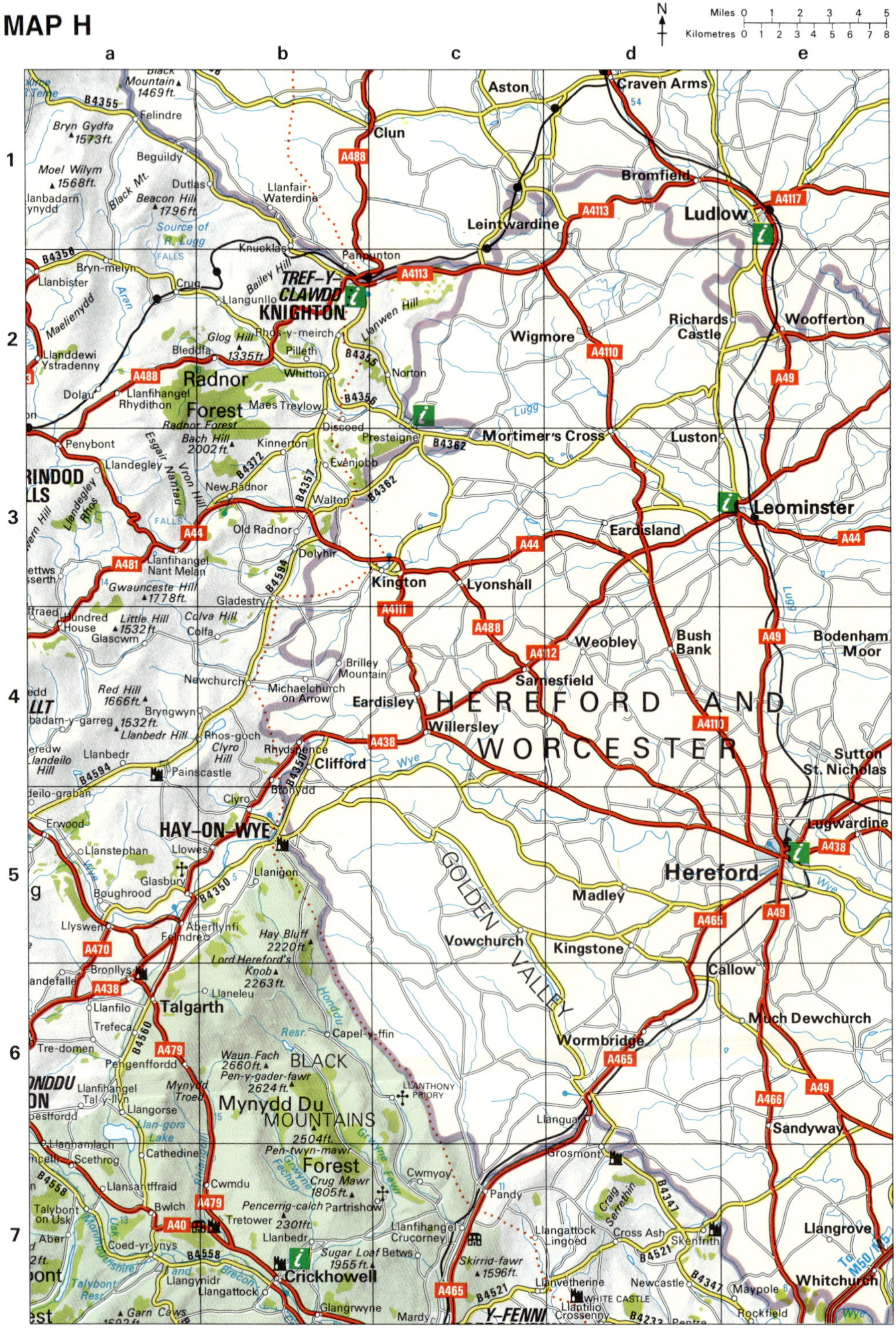

N

| Miles | 0 | 1 | 2 | 3 | 4 | 5 |
| Kilometres | 0 | 1 | 2 | 3 | 4 | 5 | 6 | 7 | 8 |

a b c d e

1

Aston
Craven Arms
54
B4355
Black Mountain 1469ft.
Bryn Gydfa 1573ft.
Felindre
Beguildy
Clun
A488
Bromfield
Moel Wilym 1568ft.
Dutlas
Black Mt.
Beacon Hill 1796ft.
Llanfair Waterdine
Leintwardine
A4113
Ludlow
A4117
lanbadarn ynydd
Source of R. Lugg
FALLS
Knucklas
Panpunton
A4113
Richards Castle
Woofferton

2

B4356
Bryn-melyn
Llanbister
Crug
TREF-Y-CLAWDD KNIGHTON
Bailey Hill
Llanwen Hill
A4113
Wigmore
A4110
Maelienydd
Aran
Llangunllo
Rhos-y-meirch
Pilleth
A49
A488
Glog Hill 1335ft.
Bleddfa
Whitton
Norton
B4355
Lugg
Luston
RINDOD LLS
Llanddewi Ystradenny
Dolau
Radnor Forest
Llanfihangel Rhydithon
Maes Treylow
B4356
Discoed
Presteigne
B4362
Mortimer's Cross

3

Penybont
Bach Hill 2002ft.
Radnor Forest
Kinnerton
Evenjobb
B4362
A44
Eardisland
Leominster
A44
Llandegley
New Radnor
A4372
B4357
Walton
B4362
Dolyhir
Kington
Lyonshall
A488
Weobley
Bush Bank
A49
Bodenham Moor
A481
Llanfihangel Nant Melan
Gwaunceste Hill 1778ft.
Gladestry
A4111
A49
Little Hill 1532ft.
Colva Hill
Colfa
A4112
Samesfield
ettws sserth
Hundred House
Glascwm
HEREFORD AND

4

Red Hill 1666ft.
Newchurch
Brilley Mountain
Michaelchurch on Arrow
Eardisley
Willersley
WORCESTER
A4110
Sutton St. Nicholas
badarn-y-garreg
Bryngwyn
Llanbedr Hill 1532ft.
Rhos-goch
Clyro Hill
Rhydspence
A438
Wye
Llandeilo Hill
B4594
Painscastle
Clifford
Clyro
Brobydd
Lugwardine
A438

5

eilo-graban
HAY-ON-WYE
Llowes
Llanigon
GOLDEN VALLEY
Hereford
g
Llanstephan
B4350
Glasbury
Aberllynfi Feindre
Madley
A465
A49
Boughrood
Hay Bluff 2220ft.
Vowchurch
Kingstone
Llyswen
Lord Hereford's Knob 2263ft.
Callow

6

A470
Bronllys
Llaneleu
Capel-y-ffin
LLANTHONY PRIORY
Wormbridge
A465
Much Dewchurch
A438
Llanfilo
Trefeca
Llaneleu
BLACK
Tre-domen
Pengenffordd
Waun-Fach 2660ft.
Pen-y-gader-fawr 2624ft.
Llangua
A466
A49
ONDDU ON
Llanfihangel Tal-y-llyn
Mynydd Troed
Mynydd Du MOUNTAINS 2504ft.
Grosmont
Sandyway
esfordd
Llangorse
lan-gors Lake
Pen-twyn-mawr
Cwmyoy

7

Hanhamlach
Scethrog
Llansantffraid
Cathedine
Cwmdu
Forest
Crug Mawr 1805ft.
Partrishow
Pandy
Craig Serrethin
Cross Ash
Skenfrith
B4558
Talybont on Usk
Bwlch
A479
Pencerrig-calch 2301ft.
Tretower
Llanbedr
Sugar Loaf Betws 1955ft.
Llanfihangel Crucorney
Llangattock lingoed
B4521
B4347
Maypole
Rockfield
Llangrove
Whitchurch
Aber
Coed-yr-ynys
B4558
Crickhowell
A465
Skirrid-fawr 1596ft.
Llanvetherine
B4521
WHITE CASTLE
B4233
Garn Caws
Llangynidr
Llangattock
Glangrwyne
Mardy
Y-FENNI
Llantilio Crossenny
Newcastle
Pentre
Wye
To A40/M5

96

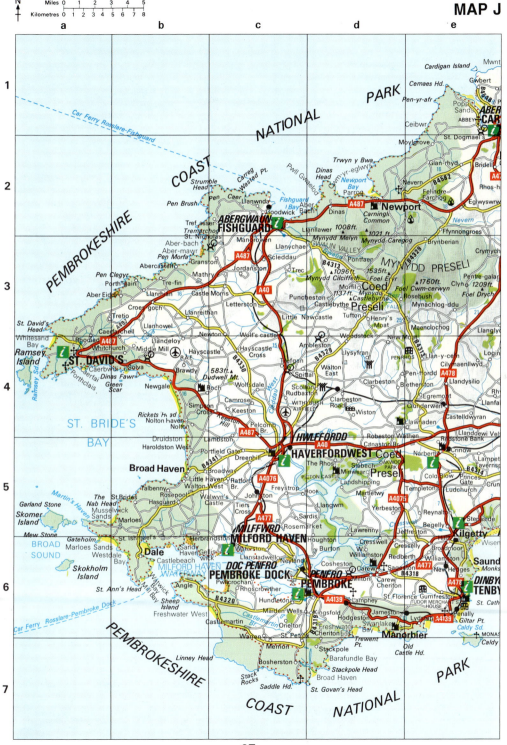

N

Miles 0 1 2 3 4 5
Kilometres 0 1 2 3 4 5 6 7 8

a · b · c · d · e

NATIONAL PARK

COAST

Cardigan Island
Mwnt
Cemaes Hd.
Pen-yr-afr
Gwbert
Poppit Sands
Aber-CAR
ABBEY
St. Dogmael's
Moylgrove
Ceibwr
Glan-rhyd
Bridell
Nevern
Rhos
Eglwyswrw

PEMBROKESHIRE

Strumble Head
Carreg
Wasted Pt.
Pwll Gwaelod
Dinas Head
Trwyn y Bwa
Trwyn-yr-eglwys
Newport Bay
Parrog
Newport
Pen Brush
Pen Caer
Goodwick
Fishguard Bay
Fishguard I Bay
Aber-Bach
Dinas
Llanllawer
Carningli Common
1008ft.
Felindre Farchog
Ffynnongroes
Brynberian

ABERGWAUN
FISHGUARD
Manorowen
Llanychaer
GWAUN VALLEY
Mynydd Melyn
1021ft.
Mynydd-Caregog
Crymych

Tref-asser
Tremarchog
St. Nicholas
Scleddau
Llanychaer
Pontfaen
1096ft.
Foel Eryr
1209ft.
Pentre-galar
Foel Drych

Aber-Bach
Pen Morfa
Granston
Jordanston
Trec
B4313
Mynydd Cilcifeth
1137ft.
Mynydd Castlebythe
1760ft.
Rosebush
Clyn
Foel Cwm-cerwyn
Foel Dyrch

MYNYDD PRESELI
Coed

PEMBROKESHIRE

Pen Clegyr
Porthgain
Abercastell
Mathry
Castle Morris
Letterston
Puncheston
Castlebythe
Preseli
Tufton
Mynachlog-ddu
Llanglyd

Aber Eiddy
Llanrhian
Llanreithan
Little Newcastle
Henry's Moat
Maenclochog
Login

St. David's Head
Tretio
Croes-goch
Llanhowel
Wolf's castle
Woodstock
New Mos
Llan-y-cefn
Llanfa

Whitesand Bay
Ramsey Island
Rhodiad
Whitchurch
ST. DAVID'S
Middle Mill
Hayscastle
Hayscastle Cross
Trefgan
Ambleston
Llysyfran
Pen-ffordd
Cilymaenllwyd
Llandysilio
Rh

Caerbwdi
Solva
R.A.F.
Brawdy
583ft.
Dudwell Mt.
Spital
Walton East
Clarbeston
Clunderwen
Llanfa

Porthclais
Dinas Fawr
Green Scar
Newgale
Roch
Wolfsdale
Rudbaxton
Clarbeston Road
Llawhaden
Egremont

ST. BRIDE'S BAY

Rickets Head
Nolton haven
Simpson Cross
Camrose
WITH BUSH AIRFIELD
Wiston
Clunderwen
Castelldwyran
Llanfa

Nolton
Keeston Hill
Pelcomb Br.
Robeston Wathen
Redstone Bank
Crinow
Lampet
Jevernay

Druidston
Haroldston West
Lambston
Dreenhill
HWLFFORDD
HAVERFORDWEST
Slebech
Narberth
Coed

Broad Haven
Portfield Gate
Broadway
Broadmoor
Minwear
Landshipping
OAKWOOD PARK
Preseli
Cold Blow
Princes Gate
Crun

Little Haven
Walton West
Ratford Br.
Freystrop
The Rhos
PILTON CASTLE
Martletwy
Templeton
Ludchurch
Col

Talbenny
Rosepool
Hasguard
Walwyn's Castle
Johnston
Hook
Llangwm
Yerbeston
A4075
Begelly
Stepaside

The Nab Head
Musselwick Sands
Marloes
Tiers Cross
Sardis
Lawrenny
Reynalt
Kilgetty
Wisen

Martin's Haven
St. Brides
Herbrandston
MILFFWRD
MILFORD HAVEN
Rosemarket
Houghton
Cresswell
Cresselly
Redberth
New Hedges
Saund
Monks

Garland Stone
Skomer Island
Gateholm
Sandy Haven
Gellis-wick
Waterston
Llanstadwell
Neyland
Burton
Williamston
Jeffreston
Williamston
A477
DINBY
TENBY

Mew Stone
BROAD SOUND
Marloes Sands
Westdale Bay
Dale
Castlebeach
Pwllcrochan
DOC PENFRO
PEMBROKE DOCK
PENFRO
PEMBROKE
Carew
Cosheston
Carew Cheriton
St. Florence
Gumfreston
Saund

Skokholm Island
St. Ann's Head
Watwick
Angle
Rhoscrowther
Milton
Jameston
TUDOR MERCHANT'S HOUSE
St. Cath

Sheep Island
Freshwater West
Hundleton
Lamphey
Kingsford
Hodgeston
Swanlake Bay
Penally
Giltar Pt.
Caldy Sd.
MONAS

Car Ferry Rosslare-Pembroke Dock
Castlemartin
Maiden Wells
Orielton
St. Petrox
Freshwater East
Manorbier
Old Castle Hd.
Caldy

PEMBROKESHIRE

Warren
Merrion
Bosherston
Stackpole
Trewent Pt.
Barafundle Bay

Linney Head
Stack Rocks
Saddle Hd.
St. Govan's Head
Stackpole Head
Broad Haven

COAST
NATIONAL PARK

97

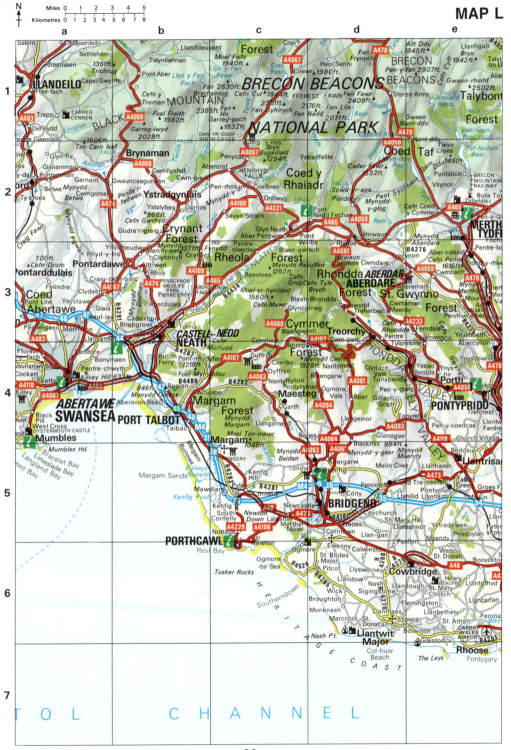

MAP L

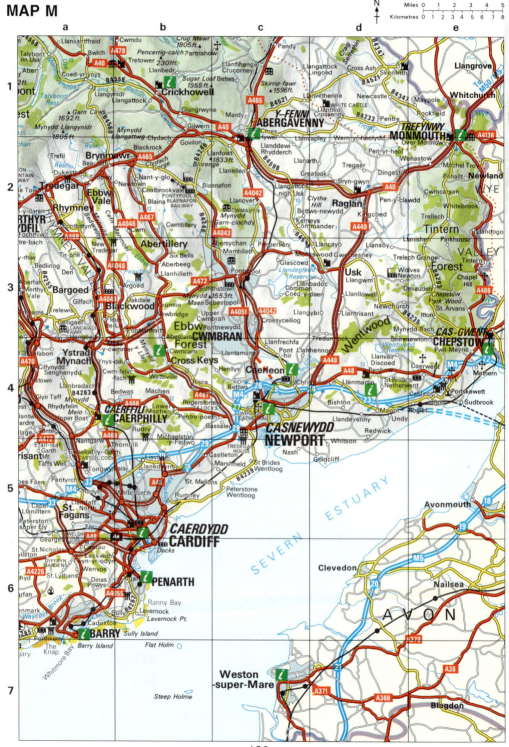

MAP M